Scran

Scrân

Modern *Scottish Food* inspired by tradition

Ali Stoner
@rovinghaggis

MITCHELL BEAZLEY

For my mum and my girls

Contents

My mum's butter knife, scratched and familiar; my gran's recipe book, handwritten and worn; the whisper of recipes muttered over kettles long before there was a cookbook on the shelf. This book is about those precious heirlooms and cherished moments – the flavour of Scotland held in hands, traditions and memories.

Introduction

There is a depth and history to Scotland's food that reaches far beyond deep-fried Mars bars or urban myths about haggis. Kitchens were humble and full of life – recipes passed by word of mouth, scraps of paper shared between friends, generations stitching together simple meals. Nothing was wasted. Cooking was shaped by whatever the land provided: peat smoke for flavour, the sea's bounty for sustenance and the garden's seasonal riches.

I grew up in Helensburgh, about 40km (25 miles) northwest of Glasgow – a town perched on the north shore of the Firth of Clyde, at the mouth of the Gareloch, with hills rising to the Highlands in the north. Over a short walk, the scenery shifts from sea-swept promenades to rolling hills with views of Loch Lomond, holding memories of beach barbecues and refreshing dips followed by 'chittery bites' that my mum had made and popped into our cold hands.

Family meals often included stovies, Scotland's nourishing bowl food made on Mondays from Sunday's leftover roast. Or a pizza supper (deep-fried pizza and chips) with the sharp smell of vinegar penetrating the newspaper wrapping, warm on my lap after a swimming lesson at the local pool. For a sugary hit, there was traditional tablet, a sweet, crumbly treat scraped from the saucer beside the stove as my mum made it. On Saturday morning walks to the paper shop with Dad, we'd return with half a dozen morning rolls, their fillings already imagined.

I'm old enough to remember those meals and lucky enough that my mum taught me how a potato, a handful of oatmeal and a bit of salt and butter could hold a story. But life changes – new ingredients arrive, we move away, time grows shorter. Sometimes those simple, comforting recipes drift out of reach. This book began as a keepsake for my children – to rescue those recipes, to record a feeling of home – but also as an invitation for others to discover what happens when memory meets invention.

Through the pages of this book, you'll find tradition – shortbread that crumbles and melts, soups that clothe the cold with smoky bones and root vegetables, puddings that whisper of childhood, lunches that carry the stories of Saturday afternoons. You'll also find reinterpretations – flavours turned a little sharper or softer, textures revisited, shapes reimagined. Then, there's creativity – recipes where I walk between worlds, drawing on old smells and new tastes, letting the memory of Scotland's larder speak in a fresh voice. My mum's influence is everywhere, but I've let my own hand reach out, too – shaped by life in Glasgow, my years in London and my new home in Australia, and by my desire to make food that feels both 'then' and 'now'.

I'm not a professional chef, I'm a home cook, who almost always chooses the effort of the kitchen over the ease of a takeaway. Wherever you cook – whether in Glasgow, London, Melbourne or under different skies – I hope these recipes bring you warmth, stir your memories and maybe even inspire you to invent something new, building your own traditions.

To build a pantry rooted in Scotland's heritage, these are the staples worth keeping close. Many have deep roots in tradition; others entered Scottish kitchens more recently, but now feel part of what we call 'Scottish food'. Use them in old ways. Reimagine them in new ones.

My Scottish Pantry

Grains and Pulses

Oats

Probably the grain most associated with Scottish cuisine, oats have been cultivated in Scotland for centuries due to their adaptability to the cool, damp climate. I mainly keep two types of oats in my pantry. First, porridge or rolled oats, which can be used in so many ways – ground to a smaller groat for quicker cooking or right down to a flour for baking. Second, and likely the one I reach for most, is fine-ground oatmeal, sometimes referred to as Scottish oatmeal or oat bran. It's incredibly versatile – great for porridge, oatcakes, breading fish or chicken and thickening stews and soups. It's a real multitasker. There are also steel-cut or pinhead oats, which I use more rarely but are brilliant for a more textural porridge, a 'ris-oat-to', or skirlie (fried oatmeal).

Barley

Barley has long-held roots in Scottish agriculture and is used predominantly in whisky-making or as animal feed. However, it remains a staple in household cookery, making a delicious base for a hearty risotto and adding substance to soups, such as Scotch broth, and stews. When ground, it's a great addition to traditional bannocks (flatbreads). The ancient form of barley known as beremeal is native to the Scottish islands and is still grown and milled in Orkney.

White Beans and Butter Beans

Beans have long provided protein when meat was scarce and are often added to hearty soups and stews. I always keep white beans and butter beans – both dried and canned – in my pantry. They're brilliant for purées and dips. My mum would often make a big bowl of butter beans, cooked in her pressure cooker, to accompany dinner, simply served with butter and black pepper. They're still a favourite of mine today.

Yellow and Green Split Peas

Dried peas were a staple in Scottish kitchens. I use yellow split peas for Pease Brose (see page 17) as a healthy breakfast alternative and they add a wonderful thick texture to my Lentil Soup (see page 70). Green split peas are also great in soups or stews. I use them for my easy mushy peas (see page 84) when marrowfat peas are hard to find.

Red Lentils

More recent in adoption, red lentils cook quickly and are the backbone of a good lentil soup. They're also commonly seen in broth mixes and are great as a thickening agent in soups and stews.

Vegetables and Alliums

Root Vegetables (Potatoes, Swede and Carrots)

Introduced between the 16th and 18th centuries, these vegetables adapted well to Scotland's climate and had a huge impact on agriculture and culinary development. They became essential in Scottish diets due to their yield and versatility – mashed, roasted, baked, in soups, stews and pies. Where would a Scottish breakfast be without tattie (potato) scones? Or haggis without neeps and tatties (swede and potatoes)? They are often used together in meal preparation, soups or stews, like a Scottish mirepoix!

Leeks, Onions and Spring Onions

These hardy alliums, often grown in kitchen gardens, are the starting point for many traditional dishes, such as stovies, mince and tatties, cock-a-leekie soup and Scotch pies. In pies and bridies (pasties), the addition of onions is often signalled by two holes in the pie lid.

Kale
For centuries, this hardy green was fundamental to the rural Scottish diet due to its ability to tolerate a cold climate. Winter gardens frequently included kale – often spelt 'kail' – which gave rise to the term kailyard. Having had a modern-day resurgence as a superfood, you can use it freely in soups, roasted or even in a salad. I love it in a pesto-like oil to dress hearty Scottish soups.

Flours, Raising Agents and Fats

Flours and Raising Agents
I always keep plain, self-raising, wholemeal and strong white bread flour in my pantry. All have their place. Self-raising is great for quick tattie scones, although these can also be made with plain flour and baking powder. Raising agents like yeast, baking powder, bicarbonate of soda and cream of tartar allow for lighter breads and cakes. Use bread flour for yeasted breads and plain flour for cakes, scones, pastry and bannocks. Combine raising agents with acid (such as vinegar or lemon juice) for an extra rise in quick bakes.

Butter, Suet, Lard, Dripping and Beef Tallow
These traditional fats enrich, add texture and deepen flavour. Use suet in steamed puddings and dumplings; butter in baking and for spreading; lard in pastry (particularly hot-water crust); and beef tallow or dripping for frying and roasting, ideal thanks to their high smoke point.

Acids

Vinegar and Lemon Juice
Acid is vital in any kitchen. It activates rising in baked goods, lightens batters and adds a balancing flourish to sauces and gravies. I keep a variety of vinegars – malt, red wine, white wine, sherry and white vinegar. Try to have at least one and always keep a lemon on hand.

Sweeteners and Syrups

Sugar, Honey, Golden Syrup, Treacle and Malt Syrup
Before cheap sugar, honey was the primary sweetener. Try to buy local honey wherever you live as it will be infused with local botanicals. When trade routes opened, sugar and syrups became widespread and the Scots developed quite a sweet tooth. Use caster sugar for baking, brown sugar for caramel notes and icing sugar for glazes. Malt syrup (from barley) adds a malty flavour – perfect in digestive biscuits. These sweeteners are useful in baking, preserving, glazes, sauces, desserts and even for balancing savoury dishes.

Dried Fruits and Mixed Peel

Dried Fruits
I don't think I ever used as much dried fruit as when I started exploring Scottish cooking. It is prolific in Scottish baking and has been used since the 17th century. Everyone has a preference – I like sultanas, currants, figs, dates and cranberries. They're largely interchangeable, depending on taste.

Mixed Peel
Oranges and lemons were also imported around the 17th century and found a place in baking, especially in the form of mixed peel. I love using citrus – even just the zest. My kitchen is constantly littered with 'bald' lemons.

Herbs and Spices

Parsley, Sage, Rosemary and Thyme
These herbs are closely associated with Scottish cooking and were traditionally grown in cottage gardens, each with symbolic meaning in folklore. It's believed the Romans brought rosemary with them when they conquered Britain. Parsley grew prolifically in my childhood garden and I now grow all four main herbs and use them freely.

Bay Leaves
I love the flavour bay leaves impart to soups, stews and oils. A Mediterranean native, bay trees are hardy enough to grow in Scotland, meaning fresh leaves on hand all year round.

Juniper
This is a native Scottish shrub, most commonly associated with gin distilling. It has a great flavour, is easy to buy dried and can be used to flavour meats, preserves and infused liquids. I use it in My Scottish 7-Spice Blend (see page 214).

Allspice, Nutmeg, Coriander, Cloves, Cinnamon, Ginger and Caraway Seeds
These spices arrived via historic trade routes and are used in puddings, cakes, festive bakes and preserves, plus in savoury dishes for warmth. Allspice was originally known as 'Jamaica pepper' and was often used as we might use black pepper today. You will find all of these in my Scottish spice blends.

Berries and Citrus Fruit

Strawberries, Raspberries and Brambles (Wild Blackberries)
I used to go berry picking with my mum, filling punnets with juicy berries and more than a few directly filling my mouth on the way. In-season Scottish berries are in a league of their own. Brambles were always picked wild but they are now easier to buy. Use berries in jams, chutneys, crumbles, desserts, cream infusions, cocktails and syrups.

Citrus Fruit
Citrus fruit add acid and fragrance to any dish. Lime, in particular, has a special Scottish connection through lime cordial. In 1867, in Leith, Scotland, Lauchlan Rose developed a method to preserve lime juice by replacing alcohol with sugar – making it more accessible and shelf-stable. (Find my recipe on page 208.)

Spirits and Infusions

Whisky
A defining Scottish spirit with centuries of history, from illicit home distilling to regulated distilleries. Use whisky in cooking, both savoury and sweet: whisky sauces, glazes, desserts like bread pudding or caramel sauce, infusions and cocktails, plus, obviously, the occasional dram on its own.

Gin
My favourite tipple. Gin distilling has had a resurgence in recent years using traditional botanicals like juniper. Use it in infusions, cocktails, syrups, dressings and pickling – try my Gin-and-Tonic Pickled Onions (see page 217).

Rum
Rum entered Scottish kitchens via trade routes in the 17th century. The sugar trade in Glasgow fuelled its popularity, leading to cocktails like the renowned Glasgow Punch (see page 210). Scots were even pioneers in distilling equipment but high duty costs made rum expensive and whisky eventually became the drink of choice. Today, local distilleries are crafting excellent Scottish rum. Use it in cocktails, sauces and marinades.

Irn-Bru
Often referred to as 'Scotland's other national drink', Irn-Bru is a distinctive orange soft drink introduced to the world in 1901. Known for its unique flavour, it is a staple in many Scottish households and is fantastic in both sweet and savoury dishes.

Scottish Breakfast

1

This is a Scottish take on a classic eggs Benedict. Layer tattie scones with sautéed kale, then take your pick from haggis, black pudding, Lorne sausage, bacon and white pudding. Any selection of these will tick all the boxes on the Scottish breakfast bingo card. Top with a soft poached egg and the crowning glory of a smoky whisky hollandaise.

Scottish Benedict with Whisky Hollandaise

Serves 4

- *Neutral oil, for frying*
- *4 slices of haggis*
- *4 slices of black pudding*
- *8 Tattie Scones (see page 22), cut into rounds*
- *150g (5½oz) kale, chopped*
- *20g (¾oz) unsalted butter*
- *Splash of vinegar*
- *8 eggs*
- *Salt and ground black pepper, to taste*
- *Cayenne pepper, to garnish*

For the whisky hollandaise

- *125g (4½oz) unsalted butter*
- *1 tablespoon Scottish whisky*
- *1 tablespoon lemon juice*
- *2 egg yolks*
- *1 tablespoon chopped chives*
- *Pinch of cayenne pepper*
- *Salt and ground black pepper, to taste*

This is a quick method, so start by making the whisky hollandaise. Melt the butter in a jug and leave to cool slightly. The milk solids will sink to the bottom and the clarified butter will remain on the top.

In a tall container, combine the whisky, lemon juice and egg yolks with a pinch of salt, and blend with a handheld immersion blender. With the motor still running, slowly pour in the melted clarified butter (stop before you reach the milk solids). The sauce will emulsify and thicken beautifully. Stir in the chopped chives and season with cayenne pepper and black pepper to taste. You can leave this to sit for 15 minutes while you cook your eggs and other elements but it is best made and eaten straight away rather than reheating.

Heat a little oil in a large frying pan over a medium–high heat and start to fry the haggis and black pudding. Toast the tattie scones at the same time.

In a separate pan, sauté the kale in the butter until softened and wilted. Season with salt.

Bring a saucepan of water with a splash of vinegar to the boil. Working one at a time, crack each egg into a small cup. Reduce the heat under the pan and carefully drop in the eggs. Bring the water back to a light simmer and poach the eggs for precisely 3 minutes. Remove the eggs immediately with a slotted spoon and drain on kitchen paper.

To serve, place a warm tattie scone on each of 4 plates and top with the sautéed kale. Add the slices of black pudding and haggis, then another tattie scone. Top each with two poached eggs, then carefully spoon some of the whisky hollandaise over the eggs. Sprinkle with a little more cayenne pepper and a grind of black pepper.

That's a good breakfast indeed.

Brose is a traditional Scottish term for cooking 'meal', such as oats or barley, with boiling milk or water. In this case, I use 'peasemeal', which is made from yellow peas. Pease meal has been eaten since Roman times but fell out of favour, replaced by the more popular oat porridge. It tends to be eaten as a savoury breakfast and is an incredibly healthy way to start the day, full of plant-based protein and fibre with a low GI.

I use yellow split peas for this recipe as they are easy to find. They are roasted before cooking to increase their nutritional value, before being ground and made into your brose. I think it's worth roasting a whole bag of split peas, then storing them for ease of use. They are easier to grind when you have more and the flour also makes great fritters.

You can top this with whatever you fancy – it's incredibly adaptable.

Pease Brose

Serves 2

- *100g (3½oz) yellow split peas*
- *600ml (20fl oz) vegetable or chicken stock*
- *30g (1oz) unsalted butter, plus an extra knob for the pease meal*
- *½ teaspoon ground nutmeg*
- *12 cherry tomatoes, halved*
- *Squeeze of lemon juice*
- *Salt and ground white and black pepper, to taste*
- *25g (scant 1oz) feta cheese, crumbled, to serve*

To garnish

- *Chilli oil*
- *Chopped parsley*

Preheat the oven to 180°C fan (400°F), Gas Mark 6.

Spread the split peas over a baking tray and lightly toast in the oven for about 15 minutes, turning halfway through, until they smell fragrant and are lightly golden. Set aside to cool, then blitz to a powder in a food processor. Store any extra peasemeal in an airtight jar.

Add the stock to a saucepan and bring to a simmer. Pour in the peasemeal slowly while whisking constantly. Keep the heat low and stir until it is cooked through and thickened. Stir through the knob of butter and nutmeg and season to taste with salt and white and black pepper.

Meanwhile, melt the 30g (1oz) butter in a separate small pan. When foaming, add the cherry tomatoes, season and leave to soften. The juices will merge with the butter to make a simple, tasty sauce. Season to taste and finish with a squeeze of lemon juice, swirling the pan to emulsify.

To serve, add the pease brose to a bowl, top with the softened tomatoes and crumbled feta, then drizzle over some chilli oil and garnish with a little chopped parsley. A fried or poached egg wouldn't be unwelcome here either!

White pudding or mealie pudding is a steamed breakfast pudding made from oatmeal, beef fat and onion. We used to call it 'Mealie Jeems'. This is an easy way to make it at home without the need for sausage skins. I steam it in a loaf tin, slice it when cool, then fry it. Believe me, the crispy edges, with soft mealie filling, topped with a poached egg, is just fabulous. It's also amazing served alongside a roast chicken with crispy potatoes. In fact, it's very similar to my chicken stuffing, so I'm not averse to throwing in some mixed dried herbs or thyme – not traditional, but tasty.

Mealie Pudding (White Pudding)

Makes about 12 slices

- *Neutral oil, for greasing*
- *150g (5½oz) beef tallow*
- *250g (9oz) fine-ground oatmeal (or oat bran)*
- *250g (9oz) grated onion (about 2 medium brown onions)*
- *500ml (18fl oz) beef stock*
- *1½ teaspoons salt*
- *½ teaspoon each of black and white pepper*
- *1 teaspoon allspice*
- *2 teaspoons mixed dried herbs (optional)*

To serve

- *Rashers of bacon*
- *Sautéed spinach*
- *A sausage*
- *Half a grilled tomato*
- *Tommy K (see page 216)*

Preheat the oven to 180°C fan (400°F), Gas Mark 6. Grease a 900g (2lb) loaf tin with a little oil.

Melt the beef tallow in a small pan, then add this to the rest of the ingredients in a large bowl and mix well. Pour into the prepared tin, cover with a layer of greaseproof paper, then place the loaf tin in a larger roasting tray filled with a kettleful of boiling water. Cover the whole thing in kitchen foil so it is well sealed and bake for 1½–2 hours.

You can eat this straight up, as it is, or cover and refrigerate. When ready to eat, cut the mealie pudding into slices about 2cm (¾ inch) thick. You can reheat it in several ways: steam, microwave or, my favourite, by frying. You won't need much fat, just a light spray, then fry the slices until crispy and golden on each side. This is not traditional, but I love the crispy edges. Simply serve with a couple of rashers of bacon, sautéed spinach, a sausage, half a grilled tomato and some Tommy K – or as part of a full Scottish breakfast.

This has Scotland written all over it! More like a burger than a sausage, as it has no casing, this square sausage is formed in a loaf tin, then cut into slices. Its place is firmly fixed on a Scottish breakfast menu – my childhood Saturday mornings nearly always started with a roll and square sausage. This is my version, heavily spiced with My Scottish 7-Spice Blend (see page 214) and a hit of cayenne pepper.

Lorne Sausage (Square Sausage)

Makes about 12 slices

- *500g (1lb 2oz) minced beef (not lean)*
- *500g (1lb 2oz) pork belly rashers, minced (or fatty minced pork)*
- *100g (3½oz) panko breadcrumbs, blitzed to a fine crumb*
- *2 teaspoons My Scottish 7-Spice Blend (see page 214)*
- *2 teaspoons My Scottish 7-Spice Salt (see page 214)*
- *1 teaspoon white pepper*
- *1 teaspoon cayenne pepper*
- *1 teaspoon ground mace*
- *175ml (6fl oz) cold water*
- *Neutral oil, for frying*

To serve (optional)

- *Morning Rolls (see page 158)*
- *Tattie Scones (see page 22)*
- *Fried eggs*
- *Tommy K (see page 216)*

Combine all the ingredients in a large bowl and mix thoroughly with your hands. I wear plastic food-safe gloves for this.

Line a 900g (2lb) loaf tin with clingfilm, leaving plenty overhanging the edges. Press the sausage mixture into the tin, pressing hard into each corner. Cover with the overhanging film and either chill in the refrigerator overnight or pop in the freezer for a couple of hours to firm up.

Take the block of sausage out of the tin and gently cut into slices ready for frying. Fry in a little oil until caramelized on each side and cooked through.

For the best breakfast, serve in a Morning Roll and add any extras you like. A Tattie Scone, a fried egg and some Tommy K would be perfect. Alternatively, try wrapping in puff pastry with a bit of Whisky Onion Jam (see page 219) for a 'square sausage' roll.

You can freeze the sausage easily by cutting it into slices and popping a wee piece of greaseproof paper between each slice. Defrost thoroughly before cooking.

Nothing beats a homemade tattie scone 'straight oot the pan'. So soft and delicious. I say ditch the bread and just make your bacon 'piece' with the tattie scones. My friend's mum used to do this for our breakfast when we stayed over. I loved staying at their house just for that epic brekkie! These scones freeze brilliantly. Dry fry them all first and then reheat in a frying pan or the toaster.

Tattie Scone and Bacon Piece

Serves 4 (makes about 10 scones)

- *1kg (2lb 4oz) potatoes, unpeeled*
- *200g (7oz) self-raising flour, plus extra for dusting*
- *30g (1oz) cold butter, plus extra to serve*
- *Neutral oil, for greasing*
- *1 teaspoon salt*
- *12–16 rashers smoked back bacon*
- *Your sauce of choice, to serve*

Score a shallow line around the circumference of each potato with a sharp knife, then place in a large saucepan of salted cold water. Bring to the boil and cook until tender. Drain the potatoes, then let them steam in the hot pan for 5 minutes. You should now be able to slip the skins off the potatoes easily. Watch your fingers as they will be steaming hot. (Keep the skins and fry them, or pop them in the air fryer with a wee spray of oil, as they make great crisps.)

Scatter 50g (1¾oz) of the flour onto your work surface. Using a potato ricer, rice the potatoes directly onto the flour. About halfway through the process, add the butter in thin slices to help it melt, then rice the remaining potatoes on top. Add the salt and another 50g (1¾oz) flour. Pull the mixture together with your hands, kneading very gently and adding as much of the remaining flour as required to obtain a soft dough. You'll need to use a little intuition as the level of flour required will be dictated by the 'wetness' of your potatoes.

Flour the work surface, cut off a piece of the dough and dust the top of it with a little more flour. Roll out to a rough circle, 5mm (¼ inch) thick. If the dough is sticky, keep sprinkling with extra flour as you need it. Repeat with the remaining dough. I sometimes cut my scones into squares to mimic slices of bread but you can also just cut each circle into 4 quarters.

Grease a frying pan very lightly with a piece of oiled kitchen paper and fry each scone on both sides until golden and blistered all over – it's essentially a dry fry. Keep warm in a tea towel while you cook the rest.

To serve, grill your bacon, butter one scone, top with bacon and your sauce of choice, then add another scone. Cut in half and get stuck in. Crispy, crunchy bacon, soft warm tattie scones...HEAVEN.

Not to be confused with the smaller, yeasted, English crumpets, these Scottish crumpets are flatter, larger and full of bubbles. Tradition would have you smother them in butter and jam, then roll up before eating. This 'posh breakfast' version sees the crumpet layered up with a spiced butter and a nippy, crabby, scrambled egg topping. As luxurious as it is tasty, this compound butter can be kept in the refrigerator for ages and is magic on toast.

Crabby 'Scottish' Crumpet

Serves 3 (makes 6 crumpets)

For the crumpets

- *125g (4½oz) plain flour*
- *15g (½oz) unsalted butter, plus an extra knob for cooking*
- *Pinch of salt*
- *1 teaspoon baking powder*
- *1 egg*
- *175ml (6fl oz) whole milk*

For the 7-spice butter

- *50g (1¾oz) unsalted butter, softened*
- *1 tablespoon chopped parsley*
- *1 tablespoon chopped chives*
- *Zest of 1 lemon*
- *Pinch of cayenne pepper*
- *Pinch of My Scottish 7-Spice Blend (see page 214)*
- *Salt and ground black pepper, to taste*

For the crabby scrambled eggs

- *1 garlic clove, crushed or finely grated*
- *1 red chilli, finely chopped (optional)*
- *250g (9oz) fresh white crab meat*
- *4 eggs*
- *Splash of whole milk or 1 teaspoon soured cream*
- *Knob of butter*
- *Salt and ground black pepper*

To garnish

- *Pinch of cayenne pepper*
- *Sprinkling of chopped parsley and chives*
- *A few sea salted crisps (optional)*

For the crumpets, place the flour in a bowl and rub in the butter until you have the texture of breadcrumbs. Sprinkle in the salt and baking powder. In a separate bowl, add the egg to the milk and lightly whisk, then mix into the flour until smooth and well combined. Leave for a few minutes – you will notice the mixture getting quite bubbly.

Heat a frying pan until hot. Rub with a knob of butter, then ladle in the crumpet batter to form 6 circles – you may need to do this in batches. Turn the heat to low and watch for all the bubbles to come to the surface and burst. Flip over and cook until golden, then remove to rest on a tea towel, covered.

For the 7-spice butter, simply blitz all the ingredients together in a small food processor, or beat by hand.

For the crabby scrambled eggs, heat 1 tablespoon of the 7-spice butter in a small pan and sauté the garlic, with the red chilli, if using. When softened, add the crab meat and lightly cook over a low heat until it is just cooked through, then remove from the heat.

Beat the eggs in a bowl with the milk or soured cream and season. Melt a knob of butter in a pan, then gently scramble your eggs. When they are still a little soft, remove from the heat and fold through most of the crab mixture, reserving a little for serving.

Generously butter the warm crumpets with the rest of the 7-spice butter, then spoon over the crabby scramble. Top with the remaining crab mixture and garnish with a pinch of cayenne pepper and a sprinkling of chopped parsley and chives. For a crunchy texture contrast, you could crumble a few salted crisps over the top.

Note: If you want to make the crumpets sweet, you can add 25g (scant 1oz) caster sugar to the batter mix. Slather in butter and jam, roll up and enjoy a cheeky breakfast dessert.

Handheld Savouries

2

There was always a pressed tongue in our refrigerator, my nana's refrigerator, and my auntie's refrigerator... ready for a 'wee tongue sandwich' at any given moment. It's probably one of my dad's favourite sandwiches. The idea of it may put some of you off but if you are a meat eater this is a delicious cut, with a melt-in-the-mouth texture. After it's been pressed and chilled, it's very easy to cut thinly. I've given it a modern take and served it 'cheeseburger style', caramelizing the tongue in a frying pan before melting over some cheese and stacking it with homemade pickles in a potato bun. This sandwich is well worth a try.

Wee Tongue Sandwich

Serves 8–10

- *1 fresh ox tongue*
- *1 onion*
- *2 celery sticks*
- *4 thin slices of fresh root ginger*
- *4 garlic cloves, peeled and bashed*
- *2 bay leaves*
- *A few sprigs of thyme*
- *A few sprigs of parsley*
- *1 sprig of rosemary*
- *1 teaspoon black peppercorns*
- *1 teaspoon coriander seeds*
- *1 teaspoon allspice berries*
- *2 teaspoons salt*
- *1 sheet of gold gelatine*
- *Neutral oil, for frying*

To serve

- *Slices of a good melting cheese, such as Comté or Gruyère*
- *Potato burger buns (or Morning Rolls, see page 158)*
- *My Scottish Salsa Verde (see below)*
- *Your favourite pickles*
- *Canned anchovies (optional)*

My Scottish Salsa Verde

- *Half a bunch of chives*
- *Small bunch of parsley*
- *Juice of ½ lemon*
- *1 tablespoon Chilli Vinegar (see page 84)*
- *4 anchovies*
- *1 heaped teaspoon capers*
- *Pinch of flaked salt*
- *Enough olive oil to blend*

Wash the tongue thoroughly in cold water, then place in a large saucepan and cover with cold water. Bring to the boil. Skim off and discard any white foam. Add all the aromatics and seasonings. Cover and leave to simmer gently for 3 hours.

Pierce the tongue with a skewer to check if it's cooked – it should go in easily. Turn the heat off and let the tongue rest in the cooking liquor for about 15 minutes.

Remove the tongue to a board (keep the cooking liquor aside). When it's just cool enough to handle, peel off the skin. You must do this when it's still warm, as it's tricky to remove when completely cool. You can also remove any gristly bits on the underside. Curl the tongue into a terrine dish. To press the tongue, I use a small round terrine dish, 17cm (6½ inches) in diameter, as it makes it easier to cut thin for sandwiches and it also makes a pleasing shape.

Soften the gelatine in some cold water, then add to 75ml (2½fl oz) of the warm tongue cooking liquor. Stir well until completely dissolved, then pour over the tongue. Cover with a piece of greaseproof paper, place a saucer over the top and weight it down (I use a can with a couple of heavy cookbooks on top). Refrigerate overnight. You can use the rest of the cooking liquor as stock for soup.

To make the salsa verde, blitz all the ingredients in a food processor and store in a jar in the refridgerator for up to two weeks.

The next day, take out the tongue and slice/shave it as thinly as you can. Heat a little oil in a frying pan and fry 3 small handfuls of the tongue slices per person until caramelized. Lay a slice of cheese on top and let it melt slightly. Lightly toast your rolls and spread with a little salsa verde. Layer on the caramelized tongue and some pickles. Top with an extra anchovy, if you like.

Cut in half and get stuck in – this is a flavour bomb!

The starting point for these smoked fish pies is basically a Cullen skink soup. I thicken it to make the pie filling. Traditional Cullen skink relies on Scottish smoked haddock for the flavour. There is just nothing else like it. The best I can get in Australia is a Shetland smoked cod, which works really well. Finish this wee pie with a grating of sharp Cheddar. Delicious.

Cullen Skink Bake

Makes 4 pies (with leftover filling)

- *15g (½oz) unsalted butter, plus a knob for frying*
- *Olive oil, for frying*
- *100g (3½oz) onions, finely chopped*
- *250g (9oz) potatoes, peeled and chopped into 1cm (½ inch) cubes*
- *200ml (7fl oz) whole milk*
- *250g (9oz) smoked haddock or smoked cod, cut into bite-sized pieces*
- *15g (½oz) plain flour*
- *1 tablespoon chopped chives*
- *1 tablespoon chopped flat-leaf parsley*
- *1 teaspoon Dijon mustard*
- *1 sheet of ready-rolled, all-butter puff or shortcrust pastry (27 × 35cm/10¾ × 14 inches)*
- *A little grated Cheddar cheese*
- *1 egg yolk mixed with a little milk*
- *Salt and ground black pepper, to taste*
- *Dressed green salad, to serve (optional)*

Heat a knob of butter and a drizzle of oil in a large saucepan over a medium heat. Add the onions with a pinch of salt and start softening them. Add the cubed potatoes, keep the heat low and sweat them together, covered with a lid, until the potato is starting to soften but is still a little hard. Pour in the milk and gently mix. Lay the fish over the top, put the lid on again and simmer until you can press the point of a knife into the potato easily. You don't want them to be mushy but to retain their shape. Carefully lift the solid pieces of fish, potato and onions out of the milk with a slotted spoon and set aside. Pour the remaining liquid into a jug.

Add the 15g (½oz) butter to the same pan and let it melt, then add the flour. Stir over a low heat to cook the flour a little, then pour in the cooking liquid and stir until thickened. Turn off the heat and carefully fold in the fish, potato and onions. Add the fresh herbs, mustard and plenty of black pepper to taste. Let it cool.

Heat the oven to 200°C fan (425°F), Gas Mark 7. Lay out the pastry and slice into 4 strips. Pile the Cullen skink mix onto one end of each strip and top with a little grated Cheddar, leaving enough room to seal round the edges and to fold over the top half of the pastry. Brush some of the egg yolk mixture around the edges and fold the top half of each pastry strip over the mixture, pressing the edges to seal. Take a fork and crimp the edges. With a sharp knife, gently make a small steam hole in the top of the pastry. Transfer to a baking sheet and brush the tops with the remaining egg yolk mixture.

Bake the pastries for 30 minutes until puffed and golden. I like to serve these simply with a sharply dressed green salad for a crunchy, vinegary contrast. You will probably have a little filling left over – perfect for an omelette or toasted sandwich the next day.

This is one of the first things my brother and I buy from the bakery when we get back to Scotland. It's just so quintessentially Scottish. I love a pie with baked beans on top, but it's probably at its best warm and held in your hand with a bit of sauce. Commonly referred to as a 'mutton' pie, it's often easier to get your hands on lamb. Ask your butcher to mince some lamb shoulder for you as it has the perfect fat-to-meat ratio for this.

Scotch Pie

Makes 4 pies

- *Broon Sauce (see page 215), to serve*

For the hot-water pastry

- *115g (4oz) lard*
- *125ml (4fl oz) boiling water*
- *250g (9oz) plain flour, plus extra for dusting*
- *½ teaspoon salt*
- *Vegetable oil, for greasing*
- *Whole milk, for brushing*

For the filling

- *Vegetable oil, for frying*
- *1 onion, finely chopped*
- *400g (14oz) minced lamb shoulder*
- *4 tablespoons beef stock*
- *1 tablespoon fine-ground oatmeal*
- *½ teaspoon white pepper*
- *½ teaspoon salt*
- *¼ teaspoon cayenne pepper*
- *¼ teaspoon ground nutmeg*
- *¼ teaspoon ground mace*

Start with the pastry. Put the lard in a small saucepan with the measured boiling water and heat until melted. Sift the flour and salt into a bowl. Make a well in the middle and pour in the melted lard mixture. Beat with a spoon until it comes together, then tip out onto the work surface and knead until smooth. Divide into 5 equal amounts, put back in the bowl, cover with clingfilm and rest for 5 minutes.

Grease and line the base of 4 deep pie tins, 10cm (4 inch) in diameter, with greaseproof paper. Taking one piece of dough at a time, roll them out with a little extra flour to about 3mm (⅛ inch) thick. Press into the pie tins and trim the edges. Use a little ball of the excess pastry to push the pastry into the corners. Roll out the fifth piece of dough and cut into circles just smaller than the diameter of the tins and cut a small circular hole in the centre of each. Chill all the pastry, uncovered, in the refrigerator for 24 hours.

For the filling, heat a little oil in a frying pan and fry the onion until softened. Set aside to cool.

Meanwhile, preheat the oven to 200°C fan (425°F), Gas Mark 7.

When the onion is cool, mix it with the minced lamb, stock, oatmeal and spices. Fry off a small piece to check the seasoning, then divide into 4 equal amounts. Place into the pie shells, then top with the pastry lids. Brush the tops with milk, then bake for 30 minutes.

Leave to rest in the tins for 5–10 minutes, then remove and serve with a good dollop of Broon Sauce.

The macaroni pie is a uniquely Scottish treat. Although macaroni cheese is popular all over the world, the Scots love to put it into a hot-water pastry shell, similar to that of the Scotch pie (see my version on page 32), then bake it. This is a substantial carb-on-carb sensation, filling but ever so comforting. I've added bacon to mine for a salty pop of flavour and used the bacon fat as the base for the cheese sauce.

Macaroni Pie

Makes 4 pies

For the hot-water pastry

- *90g (3¼oz) lard*
- *100ml (3½fl oz) boiling water*
- *200g (7oz) plain flour, plus extra for dusting*
- *½ teaspoon salt*
- *Vegetable oil, for greasing*

For the macaroni filling

- *150g (5½oz) streaky bacon, cut into small pieces*
- *2 tablespoons plain flour*
- *900ml (generous 1½ pints) semi-skimmed milk*
- *270g (9¾oz) elbow macaroni*
- *200g (7oz) grated mozzarella and Cheddar cheese mix*
- *1 heaped tablespoon crème fraîche or soured cream*
- *2 teaspoons Dijon mustard*
- *Salt and ground black pepper*

To serve

- *Grated Parmesan cheese*
- *Chopped chives*
- *Whisky Mac Hot Sauce (see page 218)*

Start with the pastry. Put the lard in a small saucepan with the measured boiling water and heat until melted. Sift the flour and salt into a bowl. Make a well in the middle and pour in the melted lard mixture. Beat with a spoon until it comes together, then tip out onto the work surface and knead until smooth. Divide into four equal amounts, put back in the bowl, cover with clingfilm and rest for 5 minutes.

Grease and line the base of four deep pie tins, 10cm (4 inch) in diameter, with greaseproof paper. Taking one piece of dough at a time, roll them out with a little extra flour to about 3mm (⅛ inch) thick. Press into the pie tins and trim the edges. Chill in the refrigerator, uncovered, overnight.

For the filling, fry off the bacon in a saucepan until it crisps up and has released its fat. Add the flour and mix well to make a roux, stirring for a couple of minutes before adding your milk. Stir well, to ensure the flour is mixed through. Bring to a simmer and add the macaroni. Stir again, cover and simmer until the sauce has thickened and the macaroni is al dente, stirring occasionally to make sure it does not stick. Add the grated cheese mix and crème fraîche or soured cream. Stir to combine, then add the mustard and season to taste, adding lots of black pepper.

Preheat the oven to 200°C fan (425°F), Gas Mark 7.

Remove the pie shells from the refrigerator and fill with the macaroni, ideally piled a little in the middle. Finish with grated Parmesan, then bake for 20–25 minutes until golden brown.

Leave for a few minutes before releasing from the pie tins. Grate some more Parmesan over the top and sprinkle with a few chives to finish, then get stuck in. This is brilliant with my Whisky Mac Hot Sauce to cut through those carbs. Then maybe go for a run!

My dad lived in Kilmarnock for many years and still supports the local football team. Killie Pie was named after and specifically made for the club, to be eaten and enjoyed at the match. It has a hot-water pastry base, a filling of chunky, slow-cooked meat and is topped with a puff-pastry lid. This is my version. I like to use venison but you can, of course, use the traditional beef if you prefer. I've even made them with kangaroo! I also like to add a piece of sharp, blue cheese, just under the pastry lid.

My 'Killie' Pie

Makes 4 pies (with leftover filling)

For the filling

- *2 tablespoons beef dripping, for frying*
- *2 small brown onions (185g/6½oz), thinly sliced*
- *4 tablespoons plain flour*
- *1 teaspoon mustard powder*
- *1 teaspoon allspice*
- *1 teaspoon white pepper*
- *1kg (2lb 4oz) venison*
- *75ml (2½fl oz) whisky*
- *Small bunch of thyme*
- *2 bay leaves*
- *750ml (generous 1¼ pints) beef stock*
- *Salt and ground black pepper*

For the hot-water pastry

- *90g (3¼oz) lard*
- *100ml (3½fl oz) boiling water*
- *200g (7oz) plain flour, plus extra for dusting*
- *½ teaspoon salt*
- *Vegetable oil, for greasing*

To finish

- *4 slices of sharp blue cheese*
- *1 sheet of ready-rolled, all-butter puff pastry*
- *1 egg, beaten, for egg wash*
- *Whisky Mac Hot Sauce (see page 218), to serve (optional)*

Heat 1 tablespoon of the beef dripping in a casserole or heavy-based ovenproof pan over a medium heat. Add the onions and a little salt and gently sauté until softened but not coloured. Remove to a bowl and add the other tablespoon of dripping to the pan. Preheat the oven to 180°C fan (400°F), Gas Mark 6.

Mix the flour and spices on a plate along with a teaspoon of salt and a good grind of black pepper. Working in batches, dust the venison in the mixture before browning in the dripping. Once all the meat is browned, deglaze the pan with the whisky, scraping up all the browned bits, then return the meat and onions to the pan. Add the herbs and beef stock, stir well and bring to the boil. Cover with a lid, transfer to the oven and cook for about 2 hours until the meat has softened and the gravy has thickened. Let it cool, then refrigerate overnight.

While the meat is cooking, make the pastry. Follow the method used for the Macaroni Pie on page 35.

Next day, preheat the oven to 200°C fan (425°F), Gas Mark 7. Fill the pie shells with the venison filling to about two-thirds full (making sure to remove the herbs). Add a slice of blue cheese on top of each pie, then top with a disc of puff pastry. Egg wash the top, cut a little steam hole, then place on a baking sheet. Bake for 25–30 minutes until golden and bubbling. Leave for a few minutes before releasing from the pie tins. Serve with my Whisky Mac Hot Sauce, if you like.

This is a slightly different take on a sausage roll, with a Scottish-spiced pork and leek filling rolled up in spiced filo pastry instead of puff. These are so light and delicious – a perfect canapé to share as finger food and even better drizzled with my Whisky Hot Honey (see page 218). My daughter loves these in her lunchbox – without the whisky, of course!

Pork and Leek Sausage Rolls

Makes 24–28 cigar rolls

For the 7-spice butter

- *250g (9oz) unsalted butter, softened*
- *1 tablespoon My Scottish 7-Spice Blend (see page 214)*
- *½ teaspoon My Scottish 7-Spice Salt (see page 214)*
- *Drizzle of olive oil*

For the filling

- *Knob of butter, for frying*
- *1 leek, washed and thinly sliced*
- *500g (1lb 2oz) minced pork*
- *3 tablespoons grated Parmesan cheese*
- *2 tablespoons fine-ground oatmeal*
- *1 heaped teaspoon My Scottish 7-Spice Blend (see page 214)*
- *½ teaspoon My Scottish 7-Spice Salt (see page 214)*

To finish

- *8–10 sheets of filo pastry*
- *Whisky Hot Honey (see page 218), to serve*

For the 7-spice butter, blend all the ingredients together and store in the refrigerator until required. Let it soften well before using.

For the filling, heat a little butter in a frying pan over a medium heat and sauté the leek until soft.

In a bowl, thoroughly mix the minced pork with the sautéed leek, Parmesan, oatmeal, spices and salt until well combined. Place the mixture into a large piping bag and cut a small hole in the end.

Preheat the oven to 200°C fan (425°F), Gas Mark 7.

Lay a filo sheet out on the work surface (keep the others covered with a tea towel while you work) and cut it into 3 long strips. Pipe a thin line of the sausage filling along a short end of each strip of pastry, then use a palette knife to spread some of the softened 7-spice butter over the remaining length of each strip. Roll up tightly into wee cigar shapes. There is no need to fold in the ends. Once you have used up all the pastry and filling, space the rolls out on a couple of large baking trays, melt a tablespoon or two of the 7-spice butter and brush a little over each roll (any leftover butter is brilliant spread on toast). Bake for 15–20 minutes until golden all over.

Serve drizzled with my Whisky Hot Honey.

This is a cheeky Scottish twist on a classic sausage roll. Named after Balmoral Castle in Aberdeenshire, Balmoral chicken is a traditional Scottish dish of chicken breast stuffed with haggis and wrapped in bacon. This recipe takes that concept and, using the addition of puff pastry, turns it into a tasty snack. Serve with a whisky peppercorn sauce for dipping, or with any other sauce you like. It makes a perfect Burns Night canapé.

Chicken Balmoral Sausage Rolls

Makes 16 small sausage rolls

For the whisky caramelized onions

- *20g (¾oz) unsalted butter*
- *1 tablespoon olive oil*
- *2 onions, halved and thinly sliced*
- *2 tablespoons whisky*
- *1 tablespoon dark brown sugar*

For the sausage rolls

- *5 chicken sausages (about 450g/1lb)*
- *200g (7oz) haggis, crumbled*
- *2 tablespoons chopped sage*
- *6 slices of prosciutto*
- *1 sheet of ready-rolled, all-butter puff pastry*
- *1 egg white whisked with 2 tablespoons milk, for egg wash*
- *Sesame seeds, for topping*

For the whisky peppercorn sauce

- *20g (¾oz) unsalted butter*
- *2 shallots or 1 small onion, finely chopped*
- *75ml (2½fl oz) whisky*
- *2 teaspoons green (or crushed black) peppercorns*
- *200ml (7fl oz) chicken stock*
- *1 teaspoon white miso paste (optional)*
- *75ml (2½fl oz) double cream*
- *Squeeze of lemon juice*
- *Salt, to taste*

To make the whisky caramelized onions, melt the butter with the olive oil in a frying pan, add the onions and gently cook over a medium heat until softened but not coloured. Increase the heat, add the whisky and let it bubble, then stir through the brown sugar. Cook until the onions are brown and caramelized. Remove from the heat and let them cool a little before making the sausage rolls. This can be done in advance.

Remove the skins from the sausages, then place the meat in a bowl with the haggis, sage and whisky caramelized onions. Squish it all together until well combined, then transfer to a piping bag. Preheat the oven to 180°C fan (400°F), Gas Mark 6.

Cut the prosciutto slices in half. Divide the pastry sheet in half lengthways and cover each half with the prosciutto slices, leaving an edge of pastry exposed. Cut a large section off the end of the piping bag and pipe a thick length of the sausage mixture along each piece of prosciutto-lined pastry. The bag should be empty when you finish. Brush the pastry edge with some of the egg wash and roll up each piece of pastry to enclose the filling. With the seam on the bottom, slice each roll into eight smaller rolls (scissors make light work of this) and arrange on a baking tray. Poke a wee steam hole in the top of each with a knife, brush the tops with the remaining egg wash and sprinkle over a few sesame seeds. Bake for 30 minutes until golden brown.

Meanwhile, make the whisky peppercorn sauce. Melt the butter in a frying pan, then add the shallots or onion and soften over a medium heat. Add the whisky to deglaze the pan and let it bubble down for a couple of minutes, then add the peppercorns and stock. Let this simmer and reduce to a thicker consistency before stirring in the miso and cream. Season to taste with salt and reduce to a good dipping consistency. Pour into a small bowl and serve alongside the sausage rolls.

The bridie is a handheld Scottish pie that originated in Forfar on the east side of Scotland, not far from Dundee. It's a semi-circular shortcrust pastry filled with minced beef and made with or without onion. One hole in the top signifies no onion, two holes signifies with onion. My version is based on tradition; I love having onion in the filling and have added a couple of extra flavour enhancers.

Bridies

Makes 4

- *Whisky Onion Jam (see page 219), to serve*

For the shortcrust pastry

- *200g (7oz) plain flour, plus extra for dusting*
- *½ teaspoon salt*
- *70g (2½oz) unsalted butter, cubed*
- *30g (1oz) beef tallow or beef dripping*
- *20g (¾oz) Parmesan cheese, grated*
- *1 egg whisked with 2 tablespoons cold water*

For the filling

- *500g (1lb 2oz) fatty minced beef*
- *1 onion, grated and juice squeezed out*
- *2 heaped teaspoons wholegrain mustard*
- *1 tablespoon fine-ground oatmeal*
- *1 teaspoon porcini mushroom powder*
- *½ teaspoon black pepper*
- *½ teaspoon white pepper*
- *¼ teaspoon salt*
- *2 tablespoons beef stock*
- *1 egg, separated (use the yolk for the filling and whisk the white with a little milk for egg wash)*
- *A heavy dash of Worcestershire sauce*

For the pastry, place the flour and salt in a bowl, add the cubed butter and crumble in the beef tallow. Rub with your fingers to a breadcrumb texture. Stir through the grated Parmesan, add the egg and water mixture, then bring together with your hands. Tip onto the work surface and gently knead to bring together in a dough. Cut into 4 equal pieces, press into small discs, wrap in clingfilm and refrigerate.

To make the filling, combine all the ingredients thoroughly and refrigerate for 15 minutes.

Preheat the oven to 180°C fan (400°F), Gas Mark 6.

On a floured work surface, roll out each piece of pastry to an oval shape, 3mm (⅛ inch) thick. Place a small handful of the filling mixture (about 125g/4½oz) on one half of each pastry oval, leaving a small border of empty pastry (you may have a little extra filling left over, which you can turn into a tasty burger!). Brush the empty border with the egg wash and fold the other half of the pastry over to enclose the filling. Press gently around the filling to seal and use a fork to crimp the edges. I use a pasta cutter to trim the edge neatly, but a sharp knife works well too. With a sharp knife cut two small steam holes in the top of each pie and place on a baking tray. Brush the tops with egg wash and bake for 30 minutes until golden and bubbling.

Remove to a wire rack to cool a little before eating with some Whisky Onion Jam.

This recipe came about when I had some of my mince and tatties left over from the recipe on page 89. I was inspired by the moment, when I was a kid, that Mum gave me some hot mince on a piece of bread as she was making it! This potato dough recipe also makes the best pizza bases, potato bread burger buns and can even be dimpled into a potato focaccia with olive oil.

Mince and Tattie Flatbreads

Makes 8

For the potato dough
- *350ml (12fl oz) lukewarm water*
- *7g packet of fast-action dried yeast*
- *10g (¼oz) brown sugar*
- *50g (1¾oz) unsalted butter*
- *600g (1lb 5oz) strong bread flour, plus extra for dusting*
- *25g (scant 1oz) milk powder*
- *10g (¼oz) salt*
- *200g (7oz) mashed potato*
- *Vegetable oil, for greasing*

For the filling
- *240g (8½oz) aged Gruyère cheese, grated*
- *500g (1lb 2oz) cooked minced beef (see Mince and Champit Tatties, page 89)*

To finish
- *Knob of butter*
- *Flaked salt*
- *Chopped chives*
- *Tommy K (see page 216) or Broon Sauce (see page 215), to serve*

Place the measured water in a bowl and stir in the yeast and brown sugar. Leave for 15 minutes until foamy.

Meanwhile, melt the butter in a small pan over a medium heat, stirring with a wooden spoon for at least 5 minutes until the butter is browned and nutty in aroma. Remove from the heat and pour into a bowl to cool.

Combine the flour, milk powder and salt in a stand mixer and briefly mix. Add the yeasty water and browned butter and mix again. Add the mashed potato spoonful by spoonful until well incorporated. Continue mixing. You want the dough to be very soft, smooth and pulling away from the edges of the bowl. It should bounce back when pressed lightly. Put into an oiled plastic bowl and cover with clingfilm. Set aside until doubled in size. You can put it in the refrigerator, covered, for an overnight prove at this point.

Tip the dough out onto the work surface and gently knead, adding a sprinkle of additional flour as required (it is a very hydrated dough, so it will be sticky). Divide into 8 portions and roll out into pizza-like discs. Top each with grated Gruyère and a couple of spoonfuls of the cooked mince, spreading it out. Fold the dough over the filling, pulling it edge by edge into the middle and pinching together. Roll lightly, then turn and roll lightly on the other side to form a flatbread.

Heat a dry frying pan until hot. One at a time, cook each flatbread on both sides. I fry each side twice and cover with a lid to make sure it's cooked through. It will take 8–10 minutes for each one.

Remove each flatbread to a board and rub all over with a knob of butter, letting it melt in. Sprinkle with flaked salt and chives, and serve with a good dollop of my Tommy K or Broon Sauce, plus a lovely martini, if you're in the mood.

On Toast

3

Kidneys featured a lot when I was a kid. My Aunt Lily made a legendary kidney soup and Mum made this dish, often served on rice, using wee chipolata sausages. It's one of the dishes that I first made when I moved away from home to study. Kidneys were cheap and, even on my student budget, I could make a hearty meal with rice, toast or a baked potato. However, it was often accompanied by complaints from my flatmates who did not share my love of offal. Poor them. They didn't know what they were missing out on.

Kidneys on Toast

Serves 2

- *4 lamb's kidneys*
- *Whole milk, for soaking*
- *2 pork or lamb sausages*
- *Vegetable oil, for frying*
- *Unsalted butter, for frying*
- *2 shallots, finely chopped*
- *10 small mushrooms, sliced*
- *2 garlic cloves, minced*
- *1–2 tablespoons sherry*
- *1 tablespoon tomato purée*
- *100ml (3½fl oz) beef stock*
- *Splash of sherry vinegar or red wine vinegar*
- *2 thick slices of sourdough, toasted*
- *Salted butter, for spreading*
- *Small handful of chopped parsley*

Cut the kidneys in half and use scissors to snip out the white sinews. Chop into pieces and soak in a little milk while you prepare the other ingredients; it will soften the flavour.

Remove the skins from the sausages and break the meat up into meatballs. Heat a little oil in a frying pan and fry off the meatballs until golden. Remove to a plate.

Fry off the kidneys in the same way and remove to the same plate.

In the same pan, add a knob of butter and soften the shallots, mushrooms and garlic. Add the sausages and kidneys back to the pan and let them sizzle up with the shallots and mushrooms, then deglaze the pan with the sherry. Add the tomato purée and beef stock, stir through and let it simmer and thicken for 5 minutes or so.

Add a splash of vinegar and stir through, then remove the pan from the heat and let it rest while you prepare your toast.

Generously butter your toast, then top with spoonfuls of the kidneys and sauce, and sprinkle with chopped parsley. The toast relaxes and yields under its flavoursome topping and makes for the tastiest, nourishing lunch.

Move over tuna melt, the Scots have arrived! Kippers are quintessentially Scottish. My great-grandfather cured and smoked herring on the Isle of Barra in the Outer Hebrides, so I feel the love of smoked fish is in my blood. Mum used to make a kipper pâté, and this is not a million miles from that process. The soft leeks and horseradish in this topping complement the strong, smoky kipper flavour so well. I also love a pickle on the side to cut through the creaminess – it's a match made in heaven, well...Scotland!

Kipper Melt

Serves 2

- *15g (½oz) unsalted butter, plus extra for spreading*
- *1 leek, washed and finely sliced*
- *40g (1½oz) cream cheese*
- *40g (1½oz) Greek yogurt*
- *20g (¾oz) capers*
- *1 heaped teaspoon creamed horseradish*
- *Zest of 1 lemon*
- *2 tablespoons chopped flat-leaf parsley*
- *2 kipper fillets (about 200g/7oz)*
- *2 thick slices of sourdough*
- *75g (2¾oz) Cheddar cheese, grated*
- *Salt and ground black pepper*
- *Pickles of your choice, to serve*

Melt the butter in a frying pan and soften the leek in the pan with a little sprinkle of salt, then let it cool.

Place the cream cheese, yogurt, capers, horseradish, lemon zest, parsley and leeks in a bowl and mix well.

Steam the kipper fillets in a steamer over boiling water, or gently poach in a little hot water, for 3–5 minutes until they flake easily. Remove the skin and break into chunks. Stir through the creamy mixture and season well with black pepper.

Heat the grill to high.

Butter the sourdough and place it butter-side down in a frying pan to toast (I like to do the other side, too). Remove to a board and spoon over the topping, spreading it right to the edges – you don't want burned crusts! Cover with the grated Cheddar, then grill until bubbling and golden.

Let your kipper melts cool for a few minutes before cutting in half and serving with pickles of your choice. A nice sharply dressed salad goes well here, too.

This is a traditional Scottish dish whose history is steeped in the ancient skill of preserving. Meats would be cooked and potted to extend their shelf life. In this case, the economical cut of beef hough, or shin, is used. It's also known as potted meat or 'potted heid'. This had a regular spot on my childhood Saturday lunch schedule, simply served on hot buttered toast with a generous grind of black pepper.

Potted Hough

Serves 8

- *1 pig's trotter*
- *1.25kg (2lb 12oz) beef hough (shin)*
- *1 onion*
- *White pepper, black pepper, salt and My Scottish 7-Spice Blend (see page 214), to taste*
- *Porridge Focaccia (see page 151), toasted, to serve*
- *Pickles of your choice, to garnish*

For the bouquet garni

- *2 bay leaves*
- *1 rosemary sprig*
- *2 thyme sprigs*
- *½ teaspoon each of coriander seeds, black peppercorns, allspice berries and juniper berries*
- *3 cloves*

For the bone marrow butter

- *Reserved bone marrow*
- *1 bulb of garlic, roasted and flesh squeezed out*
- *200g (7oz) unsalted butter, softened*
- *1 tablespoon chopped flat-leaf parsley*
- *1 teaspoon My Scottish 7-Spice Salt (see page 214), plus extra for stock*

For the parsley salad

- *2 handfuls of picked flat-leaf parsley leaves*
- *½ red onion, finely sliced*
- *1 tablespoon baby capers*
- *1 tablespoon olive oil*
- *1 teaspoon Dijon mustard*
- *1 teaspoon white wine vinegar*
- *½ teaspoon lemon juice*
- *Salt and ground black pepper*

Put the pig's trotter into a large pan and cover with cold water. Bring to the boil, then drain and dry. Cut in half (you can ask your butcher to do this for you) and add to another large pan with the beef shin.

Make up your bouquet garni by placing all the ingredients into a small piece of muslin tied up with kitchen string. Add it to the pan along with the onion, then cover with 2 litres (3½ pints) water. Bring to a simmer and skim off any impurities, then cover with a lid and simmer for 3–4 hours until the meat is fork tender.

Remove and discard the trotters and bouquet garni. Remove the meat to a bowl and the bone marrow (that was released when cooking the beef) to a separate bowl. Don't mix the bone marrow in with the beef. Strain the stock, then place it back on the heat to simmer for another 10 minutes.

To make the bone marrow butter, add all the ingredients to the bone marrow and whizz in a blender until well combined. This will keep for 2 weeks and will seriously liven up your toast.

Shred the meat thoroughly and remove any fatty bits. Season well with white pepper, black pepper, salt and My Scottish 7-Spice Blend. Trust your gut here: season and taste until it has the flavour you like.

Taste and season the stock with My Scottish 7-Spice Salt. Place the meat into a round terrine dish or bowl, about 15cm (6 inches) in diameter and ladle the stock over the meat, enough just to suspend it (you can reserve any leftover stock for soup). Cover with a lid and refrigerate overnight.

For the salad, combine the parsley, onion and capers in a bowl. In a separate bowl, whisk together the oil, mustard, vinegar and lemon juice and season to taste. Pour over the salad and toss to combine.

The next day, serve a spoonful of potted hough with sliced, toasted Porridge Focaccia, the bone marrow butter, your favourite pickles and the parsley salad.

Welsh rarebit is the well-known version, but Scotland has a version too, and the old way of referring to it is 'Scots rabbit'. 'Rabbit' morphed into 'rarebit' in later years. This is a kind of cheat's version, based on the one my mum used to make for me. There's no roux involved, it's simply a cheese paste bound with mayo and whisky (Mum would use milk when she made it for us kids). It really takes me back and I've still not learned to leave it until it has cooled, so it burns the roof of my mouth every time!

Scots Rabbit

Serves 2

For the paste

- *140g (5oz) cheese (I used smoked and vintage Cheddar), finely grated*
- *1 tablespoon mayonnaise*
- *1 tablespoon Greek/natural yogurt*
- *¼ teaspoon allspice*
- *¼ teaspoon white pepper*
- *¼ teaspoon black pepper*
- *¼ teaspoon mustard powder*
- *1 teaspoon whisky*

To serve

- *2 slices of good sourdough bread*
- *Butter and mayonnaise, for spreading*
- *Pickles of your choice*

Mix all the paste ingredients together.

Spread the pieces of sourdough with butter and mayonnaise on one side and toast, spread-side down, in a hot ovenproof frying pan until crisp and golden. You can use a burger press to ensure good contact with the pan for an even golden, toasty base.

Meanwhile, preheat the grill to high.

Top the toasts with the cheese paste on the untoasted side, spreading it to the edges, then finish under the hot grill until golden and blistered.

Remove to a board and leave for 5 minutes. Not only is it scalding hot, but the cheese paste is in a liquid state at this point and needs to rest. Cut into pieces and enjoy with your favourite pickles for breakfast, lunch, dinner or any time!

Try this alternative version with beetroot and blue cheese:

For the paste

- *1 cooked (not pickled) beetroot (around 100g/3½oz)*
- *50g (1¾oz) Cheddar cheese, grated*
- *50g (1¾oz) soft blue cheese, crumbled*
- *1 tablespoon mayonnaise*

To serve

- *2 slices of good sourdough bread*
- *Butter and mayonnaise, for spreading*
- *1 apple, julienned and mixed with the juice of 1 lemon and a pinch of salt*
- *4–6 walnuts, broken up*

Finely grate the beetroot into a bowl, then add the grated cheddar, crumbled blue cheese and the mayo. Mix thoroughly, mashing the blue cheese into the mixture until it's well combined and you have a pink paste.

Spread the pieces of sourdough with butter and mayonnaise on one side and toast, spread-side down, in a hot ovenproof frying pan until crisp and golden.

Meanwhile, preheat the grill to high.

Top the toasts with the beetroot paste on the untoasted side, spreading it to the edges, then finish under the hot grill until the top is bubbling, golden and blistered.

Remove to plates, cut in half and top with the apple and walnut pieces.

This is based on a traditional Scottish recipe that dates back to the 18th century. 'Collop' basically means a slice of meat, possibly derived from the French 'escalope'. Scotch collops are referenced in Robert Louis Stevenson's Kidnapped, *set in 1750, and it's also noted in recipe books from the same period. Collop Monday was the day prior to Shrove Tuesday (Pancake Day) and celebrated as the last time to eat meat before the Lenten period, a tradition that has now fallen away. This dish, however, shouldn't be forgotten. I've given it a modern twist to bring it right up to date. Incredibly easy. Super tasty.*

Scotch Collops

Serves 1

- *140g (5oz) venison fillet (lamb or beef can also be used)*
- *Pinch of mustard powder*
- *Beef dripping or tallow, for frying*
- *20g (¾oz) unsalted butter, plus extra for spreading*
- *4 mushrooms, sliced*
- *2 shallots, finely sliced*
- *25ml (1½ tablespoons) whisky*
- *125ml (4fl oz) beef stock*
- *1 slice of good sourdough bread*
- *Splash of double cream*
- *1 garlic clove, peeled*
- *Salt and ground black pepper, to taste*
- *Chopped flat-leaf parsley, to garnish*
- *Salad or buttered greens, to serve (optional)*

Cut the fillet into 4 pieces and beat out to about 1cm (½ inch) thick. Sprinkle some mustard powder onto each side and rub in, then do the same with salt and pepper.

Heat a little beef dripping or tallow in a frying pan until very hot and quickly sear the meat. I like mine served pink, but do cook to your liking. Remove to a plate to rest.

Add the butter to the same pan and fry the mushrooms and shallots until starting to brown and soften. Deglaze with the whisky and let it bubble and reduce, then add the beef stock. Simmer, stirring from time to time, while you toast your bread.

Add a splash of double cream to the pan, stir through and when it has reduced to a thick gravy, add the venison back to the pan. Turn the heat off and let it warm through.

Rub your toast with the raw clove of garlic, then spoon over the meat with the sauce. A quick season, a sprinkle of parsley and you are done. Serve with a salad or some buttered greens, if you like, or it's delicious just as it is.

I know sardines are not everyone's idea of a good time, but if you can get fresh sardine fillets, this simple method of cooking may just change your mind. It showcases the delicate fish brilliantly and provides such a healthy and nutritious lunch. Of course, the sardines on toast in my youth were from a tin, something I am still very partial to, but this new confit version may have won my heart and my tastebuds. A great starter option for a dinner party, these go well with my Porridge Focaccia (see page 151) or even my Skillet Oatcake (see page 148).

Confit Sardines

Serves 4

- *250ml (9 fl oz) good-quality olive oil, or as needed*
- *2 pieces of pared lemon zest*
- *1 bay leaf*
- *6 garlic cloves, peeled*
- *Small bunch of parsley*
- *20 black peppercorns*
- *12 sardine fillets*

For the horseradish crème fraîche

- *2 tablespoons crème fraîche*
- *1 heaped teaspoon creamed horseradish*
- *Zest of 1 lemon*
- *Pinch of salt*
- *Grind of black pepper*

To serve

- *Toasted slices of my Porridge Focaccia (see page 151)*
- *Ground red chillies, to garnish*
- *Gin-and-Tonic Pickled Onions (see page 217)*

Preheat the oven to 90°C fan (225°F), Gas Mark ¼.

Fill a shallow ovenproof dish about a third full with good olive oil. I like to use a glass dish, but ceramic would also work fine. Add the lemon zest, bay leaf, garlic cloves, parsley and black peppercorns, and pop into the oven to infuse for 10 minutes.

Remove the dish from the oven and add the sardine fillets, ensuring they are submerged in the oil. Pop back in the oven for 5–10 minutes until the flesh is opaque.

Meanwhile, mix together the ingredients for the horseradish crème fraîche.

To serve, spread the horseradish crème fraîche on the toast, arrange the sardines on top, sprinkle with some ground red chillies and eat straight away with my Gin-and-Tonic Pickled Onions.

Soups

4

Hotch potch, also known as 'hairst bree', is a summer harvest soup and the summery cousin of a Scotch broth (see page 75). It is light, fragrant and packed full of summer green vegetables including lettuce. Any seasonal vegetables work well here: cauliflower, mangetout, broad beans. Various cuts of lamb can be used – you could try shanks or shoulder and slow cook them in the broth. My modern take includes a grilled rack of lamb, cut into chops and divided between the bowls. A handful or two of white beans adds some substance and I like it best finished with my punchy, garlicky Carrot Top and Mint Sauce (see page 217).

Hotch Potch

Serves 6–8

For the stock

- *500g (1lb 2oz) lamb marrow bones*
- *750g (1lb 10oz) lamb neck bones*
- *1 onion, quartered*
- *2 celery sticks, roughly chopped*
- *2 carrots, roughly chopped*
- *6 garlic cloves, peeled*
- *2 bay leaves*
- *4 thyme sprigs*
- *2 rosemary sprigs*
- *1 teaspoon black peppercorns*

For the soup

- *150g (5½oz) white beans*
- *Vegetable oil, for oiling*
- *1 rack of lamb, French-trimmed, with most fat removed*
- *2 little gem lettuces*
- *Bunch of spring onions*
- *Bunch of baby carrots with tops, peeled, fronds removed and reserved*
- *4 white turnips, peeled and cut into wedges*
- *50g (1¾oz) baby peas*
- *Bunch of asparagus*
- *Juice of ½ lemon*
- *Carrot Top and Mint Sauce (optional; see page 217)*
- *Salt, to taste*

For the stock, wash the bones, put all the ingredients into a pressure cooker along with 2 litres (3½ pints) water and cook on high for 1 hour. Alternatively, cook in a covered pan on the hob over a low heat for 2–3 hours. Leave to cool, then strain into a bowl, cover and refrigerate overnight. The next day, skim the fat off the surface (you can keep this to use for frying).

To begin the soup, heat the stock and cook the white beans in it until they are tender.

Meanwhile, oil and salt the rack of lamb and grill or roast it while you are preparing the rest of the soup. I cook mine on the barbecue until medium rare (the internal temperature should be 50°C/122°F; it will come up in temperature as it rests). If you are roasting in the oven, oil it all over and sear each side in a frying pan, then pop into a preheated oven, 180°C fan (400°F), Gas Mark 6, for about 15 minutes, then make sure you leave it to rest well before carving into chops to serve.

Cut the lettuce into wedges and brush these and the spring onions with a little oil. Using a griddle or barbecue, grill the cut sides of the lettuce until lightly charred. Grill the whole spring onions in the same way, then set both aside until ready to serve.

Add the vegetables to the simmering stock – carrots and turnips first for around 10 minutes until almost tender, then the peas and asparagus for a final few minutes. Turn off the heat and add the lemon juice.

To serve, ladle the soup into bowls and top with the grilled lettuce and spring onions. Nestle a couple of lamb chops in the side of each bowl and finish with a good dollop of Carrot Top and Mint Sauce, if you like.

When I was a kid, we always had cans of oxtail soup in the cupboard for impromptu lunches or a quick dinner. Deeply rich and full of flavour, this homemade version is really like a warming stew in soup form. Packed with slow-cooked beef and a rich comforting broth, I like to serve it with some buttered, peppery, steamed root veggies on the top. As a whole meal, it ticks all the boxes and the steamed veggies give not only a lovely textural contrast, but also help cut through the richness of the stock. Serve with some Porridge Dinner Rolls (see page 152) on the side.

Oxtail Soup

Serves 4

- *1.5kg (3lb 5oz) oxtail pieces*
- *1 pig's trotter or hough (shin) bone*
- *Beef tallow, for frying*
- *3 brown onions, finely sliced*
- *3 celery sticks, thinly sliced*
- *3 carrots, peeled and thinly sliced*
- *1 bouquet garni (see page 53)*
- *1 tablespoon yeast extract (such as Marmite or Vegemite)*
- *1 bulb of garlic, halved*
- *2 litres (3½ pints) beef stock, plus about 250ml (9fl oz) extra*
- *4 carrots, peeled and cut into equal-sized chunks*
- *4 white turnips, peeled and cut into equal-sized chunks*
- *Knob of butter*
- *1 tablespoon chopped parsley*
- *Splash of sherry*
- *Splash of sherry vinegar*
- *Salt and ground black pepper, to taste*
- *Porridge Dinner Rolls (see page 152), to serve*

Wash the oxtail pieces in cold water, then dry and season well with salt. If you are using a trotter, bring to the boil in cold water, then drain and dry and cut in half (you can ask your butcher to do this for you).

Heat a little beef tallow in a large casserole dish and start gently frying the onions. Add the celery and carrots with a good pinch of salt and fry until they are starting to take on a bit of colour. Remove to a plate and set aside.

Preheat the oven to 160°C fan (350°F), Gas Mark 4.

Add some more tallow to the dish and add your oxtail. Brown the pieces well all over, then add back the veggies and the trotter or shin bone, add the bouquet garni, yeast extract and garlic, then cover with the beef stock. Place a circle of greaseproof paper on top before the lid goes on to stop too much evaporation. Bring to the boil, then put into the oven for 3 hours.

Turn the oven off and let the casserole dish cool for a while in the oven. Once cool enough to handle, remove each oxtail piece, carefully stripping the meat away and setting it aside. Strain the stock into another bowl (all veggies and bones can now be discarded). Cover and leave in the refrigerator overnight.

The next day, remove the fat from the broth (you can keep this as it makes great roast potatoes!). The broth will be very rich and thick. Add to a pan and stir through some additional beef stock to thin it out if required, before adding the reserved meat and warming through.

Meanwhile, steam the carrots and turnips in a steamer over simmering water for 6–8 minutes until tender, then toss through the butter and chopped parsley. Season with salt and pepper to taste.

Just before serving, add a splash of sherry and sherry vinegar to the soup and stir to combine. Ladle the soup into bowls and top with a pile of the steamed veggies. Serve with Porridge Dinner Rolls.

This traditional dish was given its name in the 18th century. It is a light soup in which an older fowl would have been poached for flavour. Modern interpretations include a handful of rice or barley, which you can add if you want a heartier meal. The prunes are an unusual addition but quite traditional. I prefer to remove them after they've imparted their flavour to make a tear-and-share Prune and Leek Scone to serve alongside (see page 69). Less waste, more taste.

Cock-a-Leekie

Serves 4–6

- *3 chicken leg/thigh portions (on the bone)*
- *3 leeks, washed, whites thickly sliced, greens finely sliced*
- *1 bouquet garni of 2 bay leaves, parsley and thyme sprigs*
- *10 black peppercorns*
- *1 teaspoon flaked salt*
- *1 teaspoon white pepper*
- *8 pitted prunes*
- *Bunch of chives, finely chopped*
- *Ground black pepper, to taste*
- *Squeeze of lemon juice*
- *Prune and Leek Scone (see page 69), to serve (optional)*

Place the chicken in a large pan along with the green leek tops, bouquet garni, peppercorns, flaked salt and white pepper. Cover with 2 litres (3½ pints) water, bring to the boil, then reduce the heat and simmer for 1 hour.

Add the prunes to the pan and simmer for another 10 minutes, then remove from the heat.

Leave the chicken to cool in the stock for an hour or so. Then, if making the scone on page 69, remove 6 prunes and 100g (3½oz) of the leek greens and set aside. Remove the chicken and shred the meat from the bones. Strain the stock and discard the remaining solids.

Put the soup stock back into the pan and add the sliced leek whites. Simmer until just tender, then add the chicken to warm through. Add the chopped chives and adjust the seasoning, finishing with black pepper and a squeeze of lemon juice.

Serve the soup with a warm Prune and Leek Scone, if you wish, letting everyone tear off a piece and spread it with lashings of butter.

The perfect accompaniment to a steaming bowl of my Cock-a-Leekie (see page 67) and a showstopping centrepiece for a Burns Night starter, this is my tear-and-share Prune and Leek Scone. Taking the prunes and leeks out of the stock and blending into the scone mix offers a modern and delicious alternative to eating the prunes in the soup. Serve the soup and scone together as a whole meal with lashings of butter and let your guests enjoy them while they're still warm.

Prune and Leek Scone

Makes 8 scones

- *275g (9¾oz) plain flour, plus extra for dusting*
- *1 teaspoon bicarbonate of soda*
- *2 teaspoons cream of tartar*
- *½ teaspoon salt*
- *40g (1½oz) cold unsalted butter, cubed, plus extra softened butter to serve*
- *60g (2¼oz) Parmesan cheese, finely grated (ideally, blitz in a food processor with leaves from 1 sprig of rosemary)*
- *2 heaped tablespoons chopped chives, plus extra to garnish*
- *6 pitted prunes (reserved from the soup stock on page 67)*
- *100g (3½oz) leek greens (reserved from the soup stock on page 67)*
- *150ml (5fl oz) whole milk*
- *1 egg, whisked, for egg wash*

Preheat the oven to 200°C fan (425°F), Gas Mark 7.

Sift the flour, bicarbonate of soda, cream of tartar and salt into a large bowl. Rub in the butter with your fingertips until the mixture resembles breadcrumbs. Add the Parmesan and chopped chives and mix thoroughly.

Add the prunes to a blender along with the leek greens and milk. Blend until smooth. Add to the dry ingredients and gently mix through. This is quite a wet dough, so bring it together as much as you can in the bowl. Tip out onto a well-floured silicone sheet or nonstick baking paper and sprinkle generously with flour. Gently fold together with your hands and pat into a flat round. Use a pizza cutter to divide into eight wedges.

Slip the silicone or baking paper onto a baking sheet and bake for 20 minutes, or until an inserted skewer comes out clean.

Serve spread with butter and sprinkled with chopped chives.

This was my favourite soup when growing up and it's still my favourite today. This is my mum's recipe – she would have just used a ham bone, but smoked ham houghs are easy to buy these days and yield a tasty meat, too, so that's what I use. No blending required here, as finely chopping the veg in a food processor helps them break down more in cooking and leaves a deliciously 'stick to yer ribs' bowlful.

Lentil Soup

Serves 6–8

For the stock

- *1 smoked ham hough (shin)*
- *2 small onions*
- *2 celery sticks*
- *2 carrots, unpeeled*
- *2 bay leaves*
- *Small bunch of parsley roots*
- *8–10 black peppercorns*

For the soup

- *2 onions*
- *2 carrots, peeled*
- *3 celery sticks*
- *200g (7oz) split red lentils*
- *200g (7oz) yellow split peas*
- *Salt and ground black pepper, to taste*
- *Smoked sausage, chopped (optional)*

To serve

- *Ground black pepper, to taste*
- *Flat-leaf parsley leaves*
- *Crusty bread (optional)*

Put all the stock ingredients into a pressure cooker along with 2 litres (3½ pints) water and cook on high for 1 hour. Alternatively, you can simmer the stock in a pan on the hob for at least 2 hours. Release the pressure, remove the ham hough and strain the stock into a pan. Discard the veg, shred the ham, and put the meat and the stock into the refrigerator overnight.

Remove the stock from the refrigerator, scrape off the fat and discard. Finely chop the veg for the soup in a food processor and add to the stock. Wash and drain the lentils and split peas and add these as well. Bring to the boil and simmer for about 1 hour.

Add the shredded ham to the soup and heat through. Season to taste. My mum would often chop a little smoked sausage to serve on the top to make it more substantial.

Garnish with more ground black pepper and some flat-leaf parsley. Serve with crusty bread, if you like, making a hearty, healthy and filling meal for the whole family.

This is my take on the traditional Scottish tattie soup. It's certainly a riff on leek and potato soup, but it uses a beef stock. Back in the day, water and a handful of beef mince would be used to build the stock base and add flavour and extra nutrition. I love to take that idea and add extra crispy mince on the top, with loads of black pepper! I'm sure this is one where every family has their own version, full of nostalgia, comfort and memories.

Tattie Soup

Serves 8

- *Porridge Focaccia (see page 151), to serve (optional)*

For the soup

- *Drizzle or two of olive oil*
- *1 brown onion (about 115g/4oz), thinly sliced*
- *2 leeks, washed and sliced*
- *4 carrots, sliced*
- *1kg (2lb 4oz) potatoes, peeled and chopped into chunks*
- *1 bay leaf*
- *2 litres (3½ pints) beef stock*
- *500g (1lb 2oz) minced beef*
- *Salt, ground black pepper and white pepper, to taste*

For the kale oil

- *75g (2¾oz) kale, washed*
- *½ teaspoon flaked salt*
- *1 garlic clove, peeled*
- *50ml (2fl oz) lemon juice*
- *80ml (2¾fl oz) olive oil, plus a little extra if needed*

First, make the kale oil. Put the kale in a food processor and blitz it. Add the salt, garlic, lemon juice and half of the olive oil. Pulse to combine, then add the remaining olive oil and blitz until smooth. This makes enough for a small jar. Keep it in the refrigerator for up to a week as it's also great in sandwiches.

To make the soup, heat a drizzle of olive oil in a saucepan over a medium heat and soften the onion and leeks with a pinch of salt. Add the carrots, potatoes, bay leaf and stock. Bring to the boil, then simmer gently until the veg is soft but the potatoes still retain some shape. With a spatula, push a few lumps against the side of the pan until you achieve the thickness you like.

Heat a little more olive oil in a separate pan and caramelize the minced beef until golden, crispy and delicious. Season generously with salt, black pepper and white pepper.

Ladle the soup into bowls, sprinkle over some of the peppery mince, then dot over some kale oil (you can loosen it with a little more oil to make it easier to drizzle, if needed). Try my Porridge Focaccia with the soup if you wish – it's magic slathered in butter and dipped in.

There's no clear dating of this soup as far as history is concerned, but it is likely that a pottage like this has been made in Scotland for centuries. Like many here, this is an heirloom recipe. My mum always made Scotch broth after she had made a potted hough (see page 53 for my version) and used the remainder of the beef stock as the base. Any stock here would work, but tradition would say it's started with a beef hough or lamb/mutton pieces with the bone in. Of course, you can always use a stock cube or ready-made stock instead. The lamb shanks will deepen the flavour of any stock you use.

Scotch Broth

Serves 4

- *2 lamb shanks*
- *Beef dripping or olive oil, for frying*
- *1 onion (about 130g/4¾oz), chopped*
- *2 carrots (about 120g/4¼oz), grated*
- *2 celery sticks (about 75g/2¾oz), chopped*
- *1 small swede or turnip (about 350g/12oz), grated*
- *100g (3½oz) each of split yellow peas, split green peas, split red lentils and pearl barley (you can use a 400g/14oz pack of 'soup mix' if you prefer)*
- *2 litres (3½ pints) stock (beef or lamb, homemade or shop-bought)*
- *1 bouquet garni of 2 bay leaves, parsley and thyme sprigs*
- *Salt and ground black pepper*
- *Kale Oil (see page 72), to finish*
- *Buttered toast, to serve*

Season the lamb shanks with salt and pepper. Heat a little dripping or oil in a saucepan, then sear the lamb shanks until browned all over. Add all the other ingredients, bring to the boil, then cover and simmer for an hour until the lamb is tender and the barley is soft.

Remove the lamb shanks to a plate. Shred the meat and discard the bones, then put the shredded meat back in the pot. Remove the bouquet garni and discard.

Serve in bowls with some Kale Oil drizzled over the top and a good slice of buttered toast. I serve mine with a toasted slice of my Porridge Focaccia (see page 151) and the Bone Marrow Butter from my Potted Hough (see page 53) – it's absolutely sensational.

Family Scran

5

When I was growing up, we would have meatloaf on a weekly basis. I have not altered this recipe at all, as the flavour of it just reminds me of my mum. It is deeply comforting served hot with a baked potato and cauliflower cheese. When cold, it makes a really delicious sandwich on good soft white bread or a Morning Roll (see page 158).

Mum's Meatloaf

Serves 6–8

- *1 onion, roughly chopped*
- *400g (14oz) streaky bacon*
- *500g (1lb 2oz) lean minced beef*
- *250g (9oz) lean minced pork*
- *75g (2¾oz) fresh breadcrumbs (from 2–3 slices of bread)*
- *1 tablespoon tomato purée*
- *1 egg*
- *1 teaspoon mixed dried herbs*
- *1 teaspoon salt*
- *Good grind of black pepper*
- *Vegetable oil, for oiling*

Preheat the oven to 180°C fan (400°F), Gas Mark 6.

Pop the onion and half of the bacon into a food processor and blitz until it is well broken down. Add this to a bowl with all the other ingredients, except the remaining bacon and the vegetable oil, and mix them together well with clean hands – you can wear plastic food-safe gloves for this if you prefer.

Lay the remaining bacon strips down side by side on a board or plate to form a base. Place the meat filling on top and wrap the bacon strips around it to form a log, wrapping it up like a huge pig in a blanket. Rub lightly all over with oil and place on a baking tray lined with nonstick baking paper. Roast for around 1 hour until cooked through.

You can also steam the meatloaf if you prefer. Line a 900g (2lb) loaf tin with the bacon strips, pack in the meat filling, cover with nonstick baking paper and kitchen foil, then place in a roasting tray and pour boiling water around the base to no more than half the height of the tin. Steam in the oven for 1½ hours.

Let the meatloaf rest for 15–20 minutes before slicing and serving.

Lasagne is a firm favourite in our house but this is a different take on it, once again inspired by my mum. She would often use smoked fish to reinvent dishes and this was a favourite. I've also added an extra Scottish element by making my pasta sheets with kale, but you can use shop-bought pasta if you want to make this easier. Serve with a simple salad of leafy greens, dressed with a sharp lemon dressing.

Smoked Fish Lasagne

Serves 8

- *900g (2lb) smoked fish, roughly chopped*
- *600ml (20fl oz) whole milk*
- *1 bay leaf*
- *1 onion, halved*
- *2 garlic cloves, peeled*
- *10 black peppercorns*
- *Dressed leafy green salad, to serve*

For the kale pasta

- *50g (1¾oz) kale*
- *300g (10½oz) '00' pasta flour*
- *2 eggs*
- *1 tablespoon olive oil*

For the white sauce

- *100g (3½oz) pancetta, finely chopped*
- *3 leeks, washed and thinly sliced*
- *50g (1¾oz) unsalted butter*
- *2 tablespoons plain flour*
- *2 tablespoons baby capers*
- *2 tablespoons chopped parsley*
- *Salt and ground black pepper*

For the topping

- *30g (1oz) Parmesan cheese, grated, plus extra for building the lasagne*
- *150g (5½oz) mascarpone cheese*
- *3 tablespoons whole milk*
- *Handful of fresh breadcrumbs*
- *Zest of 1 lemon*
- *Large pinch of flaked salt*
- *100g (3½oz) smoked Cheddar cheese, grated*
- *Drizzle of olive oil*

Start by making your kale pasta dough. Blanch the kale in boiling water until softened, then drain and blend to a purée.

Sift the flour into a bowl. Break the eggs in and whisk together, then add the kale purée and olive oil. Bring it together, first with a spoon, then with your hands. Knead the dough on the work surface until smooth, then wrap in clingfilm and set aside to rest.

Place the fish in a saucepan, then add the milk, bay leaf, onion halves, garlic and peppercorns. Bring to the boil, then turn off the heat and let the fish lightly cook and infuse the milk.

Sauté the pancetta in a separate saucepan until crispy and its fat has been released. Add the leeks and butter to the pan and let them soften, then stir through the flour and cook for a few minutes. Carefully remove the fish from the infused milk and set aside. Strain the aromatics from the milk, then add the milk to the leeks and pancetta and stir until thickened. Turn off the heat, season to taste and stir through the capers and parsley. Flake the cooked fish into the sauce.

Roll out your pasta sheets using a pasta machine, according to the manufacturer's instructions. I take it to number 6 on my pasta roller.

Preheat the oven to 180°C fan (400°F), Gas Mark 6.

Start to build your lasagne in a 22 × 29 × 6cm (8½ × 11½ × 2½ inch) baking dish. Start with a layer of fishy white sauce, grate a little Parmesan over, then add a layer of kale pasta. Keep layering until the dish is full and all the sauce and pasta have been used up, finishing with a pasta layer.

For the topping, blend the mascarpone with the milk and 30g (1oz) Parmesan, then pour over the top of the lasagne. Mix the breadcrumbs with the lemon zest, salt, smoked Cheddar and olive oil, then scatter over the top of the dish. Bake for about 40 minutes until golden, bubbling and delicious. Leave to rest for 5 minutes before serving the lasagne with a leafy green salad dressed with a lemony dressing.

This is a simple, at-home batter that gives the most amazing crunch to fish, fritters or even a battered sausage. No fancy ingredients required. The vinegar reacts with the bicarbonate of soda to give a light airy batter, and the added cornflour helps with that all-important crunch. Instead of serving with a tartare or chippy sauce, try my pickled onion mayo inspired by that big jar of pickled onions on the chip-shop counter.

My Chippy Batter (Potato Fritters)

Serves 4–6

- *Buttered rolls, to serve (optional)*

For potato fritters

- *2 large baking potatoes, sliced 5mm (¼ inch) thick (I use a mandolin and there's no need to peel them first)*
- *Plain flour, for dusting*
- *Vegetable oil, for deep-frying*
- *Salt*

For my chippy batter

- *75g (2¾oz) plain flour*
- *60g (2¼oz) cornflour*
- *1 teaspoon baking powder*
- *½ teaspoon salt*
- *150ml (5fl oz) cold water*
- *2 teaspoons malt vinegar*

For the pickled onion mayo

- *70g (2½oz) pickled onions, roughly chopped*
- *20g (¾oz) small capers, finely chopped*
- *1 tablespoon finely chopped parsley*
- *1 tablespoon finely chopped chives*
- *2 tablespoons mayonnaise*
- *1–2 tablespoons of the pickling vinegar from the onions*
- *Pinch of salt*

For the potato fritters, rinse and drain the potato slices, then place into pan of salted cold water. I like to use a wide sauté pan so the slices are not piled on top of each other. Bring to the boil and simmer for 5 minutes. Carefully remove the slices with a fish slice or large slotted spoon and let them steam dry on a wire rack, soaking up any excess moisture with kitchen paper placed underneath. Chill in the refrigerator while you make the batter and pickled onion mayo.

For the batter, sift the flours, baking powder and salt into a bowl, then gradually whisk in the measured water. Add the vinegar and whisk to combine.

For the pickled onion mayo, simply mix all the ingredients together in a bowl.

Take your potato slices out of the refrigerator. Place a bowl filled with flour next to your frying station and season with salt. Heat enough oil for deep-frying in a deep, heavy-based pan or a deep-fat fryer to 180°C (350°F), or until a drizzle of batter sizzles and browns immediately. Working in small batches, dip the potato slices first in the seasoned flour, then the batter and deep-fry until golden and crispy, turning as needed. I find that when they are cooked, the oil stops bubbling and is almost still – that's when you know they are ready. Remove to drain on kitchen paper, removing any crispy bits that have fallen into the oil, too. Season immediately with salt. (It's the same method, whether you're frying fish or fritters!)

Get them into a buttered roll, if you like, or serve as they are with some pickled onion mayo, and enjoy the crunch.

Now for chips. Chip shops are such a huge part of Scottish popular culture, it's hard to believe they were introduced by a Belgian in the 1870s. He spotted a gap in the market for fried potatoes and started selling chips at a stall in the Greenmarket in Dundee. They sold a dish called a Dundee buster or pea buster (or just a buster), which was hot chips served with mushy peas and vinegar. Still going strong today, this is my version. A friend of mine in London who runs a café tipped me off with the chilli vinegar and I now use it on everything. It's magic on fried fish and mince and tatties, too!

Pea Buster

Serves 2

For the mushy peas

- *200g (7oz) split green peas*
- *½ teaspoon bicarbonate of soda*
- *400ml (14fl oz) vegetable stock*
- *200g (7oz) frozen petit pois*
- *Squeeze of lemon juice*
- *20g (¾oz) butter*
- *Salt and white pepper, to taste*

For the chilli vinegar

- *5 teaspoons red chilli flakes*
- *300ml (10fl oz) malt vinegar*

For the crunchy oven chips

- *500g (1lb 2oz) good chipping potatoes, peeled (if you like) and cut into chunky chips*
- *1 tablespoon cornflour*
- *1 teaspoon My Scottish 7-Spice Blend (see page 214)*
- *2 tablespoons beef tallow or vegetable oil*
- *Salt*

First, make the mushy peas. Cover the split peas in water, add the bicarbonate of soda, cover and set aside for a minimum of 4 hours, or overnight.

Put the ingredients for the chilli vinegar in a squeezy bottle, shake and leave to infuse.

Drain the split peas and add to a pan with half of the vegetable stock. Bring them to a simmer and stir for around 20 minutes. When the split peas start to break down, add the frozen petits pois and the remaining stock and continue to simmer until everything is soft. Use a potato masher to smash the peas into the mix, adding a squeeze of lemon juice and the butter. Taste and season well with salt and white pepper.

Preheat the oven to 180°C fan (400°F), Gas Mark 6.

Place the chipped potatoes in a pan of cold water. Add 1 teaspoon salt and bring to the boil. Simmer gently until a knife goes into the potato easily but the potato does not break apart. Carefully remove with a slotted spoon to a wire rack and let them steam dry. You can keep them in the refrigerator until you are ready to roast. Before roasting, toss them in the cornflour, spice mix and ¼ teaspoon salt.

Meanwhile, place the beef tallow or oil in a roasting tin and let it heat up in the oven for a couple of minutes.

When the fat is hot, carefully add the chips to the hot oil, turning them to coat. Cook for around 45 minutes until golden, turning them halfway through cooking. Turn the oven up to 200°C fan (425°F), Gas Mark 7 about 10 minutes before the end of cooking, to allow them to really crisp up. Season with salt while they are still hot. Serve the hot chips with the mushy peas and a good slosh of chilli vinegar. You will have plenty of mushy peas left over and they will keep in the refrigerator and reheat well for up to a week.

This is the dish that my friends request the most when they come over for dinner. They are two ingredients that remind me of Scotland and my childhood. Butter beans were frequent visitors at our family table and here they feature in a hummus-style dip. Langoustines are my mum's favourite and are the perfect Scottish choice, but scampi and prawns also work well. This recipe makes the most of the whole crustacean, using the heads and shells to make a spicy oil to bring the flavours together (it's also great stirred through a seafood pasta).

Butter Beans and Langoustines

Serves 4

- *1kg (2lb 4oz) langoustines (or scampi or prawns), shells and heads on*
- *Salt and ground black pepper*
- *Sprinkle of My Scottish 7-Spice Blend (see page 214), to serve*

For the butter bean hummus

- *2 × 400g (14oz) cans of butter beans*
- *Juice of ½ lemon*
- *1 garlic clove, peeled*
- *2 tablespoons olive oil*
- *Good pinch of salt*
- *2 ice cubes, plus a little iced water, for blending*

For the shellfish oil

- *Good-quality olive oil, enough to cover the heads and shells in the pan*
- *2 garlic cloves, peeled*
- *1 bird's eye chilli, split in half*
- *½ teaspoon smoked paprika*
- *1 teaspoon My Scottish 7-Spice Blend (see page 214)*
- *Good pinch of salt*

For the marinade

- *1 tablespoon shellfish oil (see above)*
- *1 garlic clove, finely grated*
- *½ teaspoon My Scottish 7-Spice Blend (see page 214)*
- *Zest of 1 lemon*
- *1 tablespoon finely chopped parsley*
- *1 tablespoon finely chopped chives*

For the butter bean hummus, add the butter beans to a food processor along with the remaining hummus ingredients, apart from the ice cubes and water. Blend well, then add the ice cubes and blend again until smooth. Add a few additional drops of iced water to reach a creamy spreading consistency. Season to taste, cover and store in the refrigerator.

Remove the heads and shells from the langoustines and reserve. Chop the meat into bite-size pieces, place in a bowl and set aside.

To make the shellfish oil, heat a little olive oil in a large sauté pan over a medium heat. Chop up the langoustine heads and shells, add to the pan and fry until fragrant. Add the garlic, chilli, spices and salt, then almost cover in olive oil. Bring up to a simmer and cook for 5–10 minutes, occasionally using a potato masher to press the langoustine heads to release flavour. Turn the heat off and leave to cool in the pan.

When the shellfish oil is cool, strain it through a fine-mesh sieve into a bowl, pressing the heads to get all the good stuff. Strain again, if necessary, and decant into a jug or squeezy bottle. This can be stored in the refrigerator for up to a week, but do bring it to room temperature before using.

Add the marinade ingredients to the shellfish meat, give it a good mix and store in the refrigerator until needed.

When ready to serve, season the langoustine meat with a pinch of salt and black pepper and mix through. Quickly fry in a dry frying pan (you shouldn't need any more oil) until just cooked through. Spoon the butter bean hummus onto a plate, then add the cooked langoustines. Drizzle the flavoured shellfish oil over the langoustines and sprinkle a little Scottish 7-Spice Blend on the butter beans.

This is delicious served with Porridge Focaccia (see page 151), Porridge Dinner Rolls (see page 152) or my Skillet Oatcake (see page 148). I'm sure it will be a new favourite for you, too.

Loved by kids and adults alike, there is nothing simpler or more comforting than mince and tatties. It's the meal my dad insisted upon when returning home after a holiday, just to remind him he was back in Scotland. The deliciousness is in its simplicity. I use a couple of more 'modern' ingredients to create the gravy, but I still thicken it with a little fine-ground oatmeal, like my mum would have done. Champit tatties are a traditional version of mashed potatoes, but have softened spring onions beaten through after mashing.

The mince is also fabulous served on toast. Known in Scotland as mince collops, we used to have this on a Saturday lunchtime. Check out my Mince and Tattie Flatbreads (see page 44) to use up any leftovers, although it's so good you might just need to make another batch.

Mince and Champit Tatties

Serves 4

For the champit tatties

- *Bunch of spring onions, finely sliced*
- *100g (3½oz) butter, plus a knob for the spring onions and extra to serve*
- *1.3kg (3lb) potatoes, peeled and chopped into small chunks*
- *250ml (9fl oz) whole milk*
- *½ teaspoon salt*
- *Ground black pepper*

For the mince

- *1 large brown onion, chopped*
- *1 tablespoon neutral oil*
- *500g (1lb 2oz) minced beef*
- *4 carrots, diced*
- *200ml (7fl oz) beef stock*
- *1 tablespoon soy sauce*
- *1 tablespoon yeast extract (such as Marmite or Vegemite)*
- *1 tablespoon fine-ground oatmeal, to thicken*
- *Salt and ground black pepper*

To serve

- *Cooked peas*
- *Knob of butter*

For the champit tatties, add the spring onions to a small frying pan with a knob of butter and gently sauté until they have softened. Put aside until the potatoes are ready.

Place the potatoes in a large saucepan of salted cold water and bring to the boil. Cook until very tender, then drain and place them back in the hot pan.

In a small pan, warm the milk and 100g (3½oz) butter together. When simmering, pour into your potatoes. Give them a good mash, making sure there are no lumps. Add the salt and beat with a wooden spoon until smooth and creamy. Now add your softened spring onions and beat once again. Check for seasoning and adjust as necessary. Keep warm.

For the mince, sauté the onion in the oil until soft, then add the minced beef, breaking it up and cooking until browned. Add the carrots and stock and bring to a simmer, then add the soy sauce and yeast extract and continue to simmer until the carrots are tender. Sprinkle the surface with the oatmeal and stir. Continue to cook gently until the liquid has been absorbed and the mince is coated in a lovely thick gravy. Season to taste.

I like to serve a few peas alongside and put an extra knob of butter on my mash with a hefty grind of black pepper.

This recipe combines my Scottish heritage with my life in Australia. My mother-in-law, Christina, taught me how to make Scotch eggs. Hers are legendary. This is a play on the famous Asian son-in-law eggs, a dish I ate for the first time in Melbourne. It's a Scotch egg with Asian overtones, using prawns for the coating instead of sausage, served with a sticky tamarind sauce and a spicy mayonnaise (see photograph overleaf). The combination of flavours is sensational.

Daughter-in-Law Scotch Eggs

Makes 5

- *5 eggs*
- *Vegetable oil, for deep-frying*
- *Ground black pepper, to garnish*

For the prawn paste

- *450g (1lb) raw peeled prawns*
- *1 egg white*
- *1 bird's eye chilli (or other hot red chilli), finely chopped*
- *3 spring onions, finely chopped*
- *Stalks from a bunch of coriander, finely chopped*
- *1 large garlic clove, finely grated*
- *Thumb-sized piece fresh root ginger, peeled*
- *Zest of 1 lime*
- *1 teaspoon white pepper*
- *½ teaspoon salt*

For the coating

- *4 tablespoons plain flour*
- *4 tablespoons mayonnaise*
- *4 tablespoons whole milk*
- *100g (3½oz) panko breadcrumbs*
- *Salt*

First, soft-boil your eggs. Bring a saucepan of water to the boil, carefully place the eggs in and bring back to the boil, then immediately set a timer for 4 minutes. Have a bowl of iced water ready. When the timer goes off, lift the eggs out and plunge them immediately into the cold water. Leave to cool.

In a food processor, combine all the ingredients for the prawn paste and blitz quickly just until it all comes together. Don't overwork it.

For the coating, fill a shallow bowl with the flour and season with salt. Place the mayonnaise in a second bowl and mix in the milk. Fill a third bowl with the panko breadcrumbs. Now peel the eggs, but very carefully, as the yolks will still be soft. Divide the prawn paste into five portions. Wet your hands and flatten a portion, about one fifth, of the prawn paste in one hand, then place an egg on top (I wear plastic food-safe gloves for this). Carefully mould the prawn paste to cover the egg entirely. Roll it in the seasoned flour and set aside on a piece of greaseproof paper sprinkled with a little more seasoned flour. Cover all the eggs in this way. One at a time, dip and cover each egg in the milk and mayo mixture, then roll them in the panko breadcrumbs until coated. You can keep these in the refrigerator until you are ready to fry.

For the tamarind sauce

- *100g (3½oz) concentrated palm sugar*
- *40g (1½oz) dark brown sugar*
- *60ml (4 tablespoons) fish sauce*
- *100g (3½oz) tamarind purée*
- *1 bird's eye chilli, finely chopped*
- *Juice of ½ lime*

For the chilli mayo

- *3 tablespoons mayonnaise*
- *1 tablespoon crispy chilli oil (shop-bought)*
- *Juice of ½ lime*

To serve

- *Crunchy lettuce leaves*
- *Lime quarters*

To make the tamarind sauce, combine all the ingredients except the lime juice in a saucepan. Add 4 tablespoons water and simmer until thickened, then turn off the heat and stir through the lime juice.

For the chilli mayo, just combine all the ingredients in a small bowl.

When you are ready to cook, heat enough oil for deep-frying in a deep, heavy pan or deep-fat fryer to 180°C (350°F), or until a cube of bread browns in 30 seconds. Deep-fry the Scotch eggs two at a time, turning until they are golden all over. Remove to drain on kitchen paper while you cook the others.

Serve in lettuce-leaf cups, garnished with ground black pepper and with the sauces and lime quarters on the side for squeezing over. You can eat these with a knife and fork, or get your hands messy by quartering the eggs, placing a piece in a lettuce-leaf cup, then topping with the sauces and eating in one bite. They are so good!

I love this way of cooking lamb. Not only is it delicious but it's a bit of a showstopper dish for a dinner party. It can all be prepped the day before, then cooked to order. I love serving this as a deconstructed Scotch broth with a pearl barley 'risotto' and Punchy Parsley Sauce (see page 216).

Pressed Lamb

Serves 8

- *2.25kg (5lb) lamb shoulder on the bone*
- *Handful of rosemary sprigs*
- *Handful of thyme sprigs*
- *Olive oil, for frying*
- *Punchy Parsley Sauce (see page 216), to serve*

For the lamb marinade

- *1 tablespoon toasted coriander seeds*
- *1 teaspoon flaked salt*
- *6 garlic cloves, peeled*
- *1 teaspoon ground black pepper*
- *1 teaspoon ground nutmeg*
- *1 teaspoon ground allspice*
- *2 teaspoons dried thyme*
- *Drizzle of olive oil*

For the pearl barley 'risotto'

- *Olive oil, for frying*
- *½ onion, finely chopped*
- *1 celery stick, finely chopped*
- *1 carrot, finely chopped*
- *1 garlic clove, finely grated*
- *150g (5½oz) pearl barley, rinsed*
- *Splash of vermouth or white wine*
- *1 bay leaf*
- *600ml (20fl oz) vegetable stock*
- *Handful of kale, blanched and chopped*
- *30g (1oz) butter*
- *Squeeze of lemon juice*
- *Salt and ground white and black pepper*

Preheat the oven to 160°C fan (350°F), Gas Mark 4.

To make the marinade, crush the coriander seeds in a pestle and mortar, add the salt and keep crushing, then add the garlic and crush to a pulp. Add all the spices and the thyme with a drizzle of olive oil and mix to a paste. Using a sharp knife, score the lamb on the fatty side in a crosshatched pattern, then rub the marinade all over. Place in a large roasting tin, resting it on a bed of the rosemary and thyme sprigs, then cover with greaseproof paper and a double layer of kitchen foil. Roast for 4 hours.

Once the lamb is cooked, remove from the oven, reserve the bones, discard any fatty bits and then shred all the meat with a couple of forks. Transfer the shredded meat to a small roasting tin lined with clingfilm. Drain the cooking juices from the large tin and remove the fat, then mix half of the juices through the shredded lamb (reserve the rest of the juices for making the jus) and press well into the tin. Cover with greaseproof paper and weight heavily with another roasting tin and put a heavy book on top. Chill in the refrigerator overnight.

Next day, remove the lamb from the tin, cut the edges off (these can be used to make a crispy lamb salad) and cut into eight portions.

To make the 'risotto', heat a little olive oil in a sauté pan and soften the onion, celery and carrot. Add the garlic and sauté for a minute, then add the barley to the pan with a splash of vermouth or white wine. Stir until the liquid has been absorbed. Season with a little salt, add the bay leaf, then add half of the stock. Stir and cover with a lid. Once the liquid has been absorbed, add the rest of the stock. When that is nearly absorbed, add the kale, season to taste, then add the butter and a squeeze of lemon juice. Stir, cover and leave to rest.

For the lamb jus

- *1kg (2lb 4oz) additional lamb bones (ask your butcher)*
- *2 onions, quartered*
- *2 carrots, cut into chunky slices*
- *Bunch of celery tops, or 2 celery sticks, cut into chunky slices*
- *Few sprigs of thyme*
- *1 bay leaf*
- *6 garlic cloves, peeled*
- *1 litre (1¾ pints) chicken stock*
- *250ml (9fl oz) red wine*
- *30g (1oz) unsalted butter, cubed*

To make a lamb stock for the jus, I use a pressure cooker for speed. First, roast the additional bones with 1 onion for colour at 200°C (425°F), Gas mark 7 for about 30 minutes. Add the reserved lamb shoulder bones, the reserved lamb cooking juices and the second onion along with all the other lamb jus ingredients, except the butter, to the pressure cooker and cook for 1 hour. If you are making it on the hob, bring to the boil and then reduce the heat and leave to simmer for 2–3 hours over a low heat. Strain the stock into a saucepan and reduce over a high heat until thick and syrupy. To finish, whisk in the butter, cube by cube, until incorporated and the sauce is glossy, then cover until ready to serve.

When you have everything else prepped and ready, heat a little oil in a frying pan and fry the lamb portions quickly on both sides, creating crispy edges. Use a palette knife and carefully lift out to a plate – although the crispy edges will hold the portions together, they will be meltingly tender within and can easily fall apart. This needs to be done right at the last minute and served straight away – don't leave them sitting in the pan as they may fall apart. Serve drizzled with the lamb jus alongside the pearl barley 'risotto'. Finish with the punchy parsley sauce (see photograph on previous page).

There's never a complaint when fish pie is on the menu in our house, and it's sure to be a crowd-pleaser in yours. Comforting and easy, if the weather's a bit grey or you just want some comfort food, this dish has your back. You can use any selection of fish you like. Smoked fish is great, especially if you live in Scotland where it's full of flavour.

Fish Pie

Serves 4–6

- *50g (1¾oz) unsalted butter*
- *1 leek, washed and finely chopped*
- *100ml (3½fl oz) white wine*
- *1 bay leaf*
- *40g (1½oz) plain flour*
- *500ml (18fl oz) whole milk*
- *2 teaspoons Dijon mustard*
- *1 tablespoon baby capers*
- *2 tablespoons chopped chives*
- *2 tablespoons chopped parsley*
- *800g (1lb 12oz) mixed raw fish, chopped into bite-sized chunks*
- *8 large, peeled raw king prawns*
- *3 hard-boiled eggs, peeled and quartered*
- *Salt and ground black pepper*
- *Buttered peas, to serve (optional)*

For the mash

- *1kg (2lb 4oz) potatoes*
- *100ml (3½fl oz) whole milk*
- *50g (1¾oz) unsalted butter, plus an extra 100g (3½oz), melted*
- *1 tablespoon Dijon mustard*
- *1 tablespoon wholegrain mustard*
- *2 egg yolks*
- *Salt and ground black pepper*

Melt the butter in a large saucepan over a medium heat and soften the leek. Add the white wine and bay leaf and bubble until nearly evaporated, then sprinkle over the flour, stir through and cook for a few minutes. Add the milk and stir until thickened, then add the mustard, capers and chopped herbs. Season to taste, cover and leave to cool.

You can make your mash any way you like, but I cook my potatoes in the skins whole, then push them through a sieve for a silky, lump-free mash. Warm the milk and 50g (1¾oz) butter and beat through the mash, then beat in the mustards and egg yolks, adjusting the seasoning if required. Pop into a piping bag fitted with a large star nozzle for lovely crispy ridges (this is optional).

Preheat the oven to 180°C fan (400°F), Gas Mark 6.

Stir the fish and prawns through the cooled sauce and transfer to a large ovenproof dish. Arrange the hard-boiled egg quarters over the surface and season lightly. Pipe the mash over the top (or just pile the mash on and rough the surface with a fork), then drizzle over the melted butter. Bake for about 40 minutes until bubbling and golden brown all over.

Serve with buttered peas, if you like.

A classic Scottish steak pie is a stew with a pastry lid, but we still call it a pie. When the rain is battering the windows, the smell of this cooking is a joy. It's popular for a Burns Night dinner and traditional in Scotland for New Year's Day, perhaps to soak up the revelry from the night before. This is what may be called the 'Lanarkshire' version, which includes sausages in bite-sized pieces.

Steak Pie

Serves 4

- *2 tablespoons beef dripping or neutral oil*
- *1 brown onion, thinly sliced*
- *3 celery sticks, finely chopped*
- *3 garlic cloves, thinly sliced*
- *4 carrots, thinly sliced*
- *1 bouquet garni of 1 bay leaf and a small bunch of thyme*
- *6 beef sausages*
- *1 tablespoon plain flour*
- *1 teaspoon onion powder*
- *1 teaspoon ground allspice*
- *500g (1lb 2oz) stewing steak*
- *300ml (10fl oz) beef stock*
- *1 × 300ml (10fl oz) can of stout (I use oatmeal stout)*
- *1 sheet of ready-rolled, all-butter puff pastry*
- *1 egg, beaten, for egg wash*
- *Salt*
- *Buttery mash and veggies, to serve (optional)*

Heat half of the dripping in an ovenproof pan and sauté the onion and celery with a pinch of salt until softened. Add the garlic, carrots and bouquet garni, sauté for 5 minutes, then remove from the pan to a bowl and set aside.

Remove the skin from the sausages and break into bite-sized pieces. Brown them in the same pan, then remove to the bowl and set aside.

Preheat the oven to 170°C fan (375°F), Gas Mark 5.

In a bowl, mix together the plain flour, onion powder and allspice with 1 teaspoon salt. Toss the stewing steak through the mixture until well coated. In the same pan, melt the rest of the dripping and fry the steak in batches until browned, then add the sausages and veg back to the pan. Add the stock and stout and bring to the boil, then cover with a lid and cook in the oven for 2 hours.

After this time, remove the bouquet garni, adjust the seasoning if required, and transfer to a 26 × 19 × 6cm (10½ × 7½ × 2½ inch) pie dish. Increase the oven temperature to 180°C fan (400°F), Gas Mark 6.

Cover the pie dish with the sheet of puff pastry and trim the edges with a sharp knife. You can use the offcuts to make a design on the top. Make two small steam holes in the pastry, brush with beaten egg and bake for around 25 minutes until golden and crispy.

Serve with buttery mash and veggies, if you like.

I often make a veggie haggis, mainly for my English and Australian pals who are scared by the real deal. This really does replicate the original in flavour, texture and looks. It also makes a brilliant filling for 'sausage' rolls, a perfect dinner option that I serve for vegetarian guests.

Vegetarian Haggis

Serves 6

- *15g (½oz) dried mushrooms (porcini or shiitake), diced*
- *2 tablespoons olive oil*
- *25g (scant 1oz) butter*
- *1 brown onion, finely chopped*
- *2 garlic cloves, minced*
- *4 portobello mushrooms, diced*
- *2 teaspoons My Scottish 7-Spice Blend (see page 214)*
- *1 teaspoon white pepper*
- *½ teaspoon ground mace*
- *2 sprigs of sage, leaves finely chopped*
- *1 sprig of rosemary, leaves finely chopped*
- *2 carrots, very finely diced (I use a food processor)*
- *75g (2¾oz) black beluga lentils*
- *1 tablespoon yeast extract (such as Marmite or Vegemite)*
- *500ml (18fl oz) vegetable stock*
- *1 × 400g (14oz) can white beans, drained and chopped*
- *Zest of 1 lemon*
- *50g (1¾oz) steel-cut or pinhead oats*
- *Salt*

To serve

- *Champit Tatties (see page 89)*
- *Mashed cooked swede*
- *Whisky Onion Jam (see page 219), warmed*

Rehydrate the dried mushrooms by covering in about 100ml (3½fl oz) boiling water and leaving for 15 minutes.

Heat the oil and butter in a saucepan, then add the onion and garlic and start to soften. Add the fresh mushrooms to the pan, followed by the rehydrated dried mushrooms (reserving the soaking liquor). When softened, add the spices, herbs, carrot, lentils, yeast extract, mushroom liquor and 400ml (14fl oz) of the stock. Simmer, stirring frequently, for about 30 minutes until the lentils are almost softened.

Add the beans and lemon zest to the mix along with ½ teaspoon salt. Test the lentils for 'doneness' and add the rest of the stock if the lentils require more cooking – they should still retain a little bite and most of the liquid should have been absorbed. Add the oats and let them absorb the remaining liquid. Taste and add more salt, if required.

Serve with a spoonful of Champit Tatties, a spoonful of mashed neeps (swede) and some of my warm Whisky Onion Jam.

I know this sounds like a joke but bear with me as it really works. Cooking gammon in fizzy drinks is not a new thing – cola, ginger ale, beer...they all work. The sweetness balances the saltiness of the gammon, resulting in tender, flavoursome meat, then the liquor is reduced to make a sticky glaze before the meat is roasted until it's golden and caramelized. This Scottish take on ham is sure to be a crowd-pleaser at Christmas or indeed any time.

Irn-Bru Ham

Serves 10–12

- *3kg (6lb 8oz) gammon joint*
- *2 litres (3½ pints) Irn-Bru*
- *150ml (5fl oz) apple juice (fresh or good-quality shop-bought)*
- *5 cloves*
- *1 teaspoon coriander seeds*
- *1 teaspoon black peppercorns*
- *1 teaspoon allspice berries*
- *1 blade of mace (or 1 teaspoon ground mace)*
- *1 bay leaf*

For the glaze

- *150ml (5fl oz) apple juice (fresh or good-quality shop-bought)*
- *2 heaped teaspoons wholegrain mustard*

To serve (optional)

- *2 tablespoons mayonnaise*
- *Squeeze of lemon juice*
- *Porridge Focaccia (see page 151)*
- *Peppercorn Cheddar cheese, grated*
- *Crunchy lettuce leaves*

Add the gammon, all the liquid and the spices to a large lidded pot and bring to the boil, then cover and reduce to a simmer. Cook for 2¼ hours (roughly 45 minutes per kilogram), turning the gammon halfway through cooking. It's going to look a bit unappetizing, but that's what the glazing step is for.

Remove the gammon to a board (reserve the cooking liquor) and cut off the string and the rind, leaving the fat attached. Score the fat in a diagonal crosshatched pattern, then place the joint in a roasting tray.

Preheat the oven to 200°C fan (425°F), Gas Mark 7.

Next, prepare the glaze. Measure 200ml (7fl oz) of the cooking liquor into a small saucepan and add the apple juice. Bring to the boil and reduce the liquor until it resembles a thick caramel, then stir in the mustard. Mix well, then baste the ham all over with the glaze. Place the the ham in the oven for 15 minutes.

Meanwhile, preheat the grill to hot.

Remove the ham from the oven, baste again with the glaze and finish under the grill until caramelized and golden. Let it cool before carving.

This is great served in a sandwich. Just mix any remaining glaze with 2 tablespoons mayonnaise and a squeeze of lemon juice, then use that to make a sandwich with the ham, my Porridge Focaccia and maybe some peppercorn Cheddar. The flavour is fantastic!

This dish takes me back to my school days, although this version is way tastier. Contrary to the name, it contains no olives – it's beef steak wrapped around a tasty filling. Back in my gran's day, the meat would have been filled with an oatmeal stuffing, but as the years progressed it was replaced with sausage meat. I have made a hybrid version using minced pork and oatmeal for a flavoursome filling. This is gorgeous served with Clapshot (see page 116) and some simple steamed greens.

Beef Olives

Serves 4

- *4 × 140–150g (5–5½oz) pieces of beef chuck or skirt*
- *1–2 tablespoons beef dripping*
- *160g (5¾oz) onion, finely diced*
- *160g (5¾oz) carrots, finely diced*
- *140g (5oz) celery, finely diced*
- *2 garlic cloves, crushed*
- *1 heaped tablespoon plain flour*
- *500ml (18fl oz) beef stock*
- *500ml (18fl oz) beer*
- *2 sprigs of rosemary*
- *1 bay leaf*
- *1 tablespoon porcini powder*
- *1 tablespoon soy sauce*
- *Splash of red wine vinegar*
- *Zest of 1 lemon*
- *Salt*

For the stuffing

- *3 tablespoons beef dripping*
- *1 large onion (about 150g/5½oz), finely chopped*
- *100g (3½oz) streaky bacon, finely chopped*
- *70g (2½oz) oatmeal*
- *1 teaspoon mustard powder*
- *1 teaspoon white pepper*
- *1 teaspoon black pepper*
- *Few sprigs of thyme*
- *2 tablespoons chopped chives*
- *2 tablespoons chopped parsley*
- *150g (5½oz) minced pork*

To serve

- *Clapshot (see page 116)*
- *Steamed greens, such as broccoli*

First, make the stuffing. Heat the beef dripping in a frying pan and soften the onions, then add the bacon and let most of the fat render out. Stir through the oatmeal, seasonings and herbs, then remove from the heat and allow to cool.

When cool, mix in the minced pork, giving it a good squish with your hands, then divide into four sausage shapes.

Flatten each piece of beef with a tenderizing mallet until they are about 5mm (¼ inch) thick. Take a stuffing portion, roll a slice of beef around it to enclose and secure with some kitchen string. Repeat to make four parcels.

Preheat the oven to 170°C fan (375°F), Gas Mark 5.

Heat a little more beef dripping in a lidded casserole dish and sear the parcels on each side. Remove and set aside. Add the onion, carrots and celery to the pan with more dripping, if required, and a pinch of salt. Fry until beginning to soften, then add the garlic. Stir the flour into the pan and let it cook out for a few minutes before adding the stock and beer along with the rosemary and bay leaf. Stir in the porcini powder and soy sauce, then place the beef parcels into the sauce. Cover with a greaseproof paper cartouche (this is basically just a circle of greaseproof paper), then the lid and cook in the oven for 2 hours. Remove the cartouche after 1 hour and turn the parcels. Remove the lid for the last 20 minutes of cooking.

Remove the beef parcels from the dish and discard the string. Discard the herbs from the sauce and finish with a splash of red wine vinegar and the lemon zest, stirring it through.

Serve the beef olives with Clapshot and steamed greens.

Tacos are eaten on repeat in my house and these smash tacos with a Scottish accent showcase two of my favourite Scottish ingredients – scallops and black pudding. A true taste of home, tattie scones are the perfect vehicle for delicious soft tacos. Serve with Gin-and-Tonic Pickled Onions (see page 217) and Whisky Mac Hot Sauce (see page 218).

Tattie Scone Tacos

Serves 4

For the tattie scones

- *1kg (2lb 4oz) potatoes, unpeeled*
- *200g (7oz) self-raising flour, plus extra for dusting*
- *30g (1oz) cold butter, thinly sliced*
- *Vegetable oil, for frying*
- *Salt*

For the filling

- *500g (1lb 2oz) scallops, roe removed*
- *1 bird's eye chilli, finely chopped, plus extra to garnish*
- *2 tablespoons finely chopped chives*
- *1 tablespoon finely chopped parsley, plus extra parsley leaves to garnish*
- *Zest of 1 lemon*
- *1 garlic clove, finely grated*
- *1 teaspoon ground coriander*
- *Salt and ground black pepper*

For the slaw

- *1 teaspoon Dijon mustard*
- *2 tablespoons lemon juice*
- *2 tablespoons olive oil*
- *¼ white or Savoy cabbage, finely shredded*
- *1 green apple (Granny Smith), julienned*
- *1 tablespoon finely chopped chives*
- *Salt*

To serve

- *Black pudding*
- *Gin-and-Tonic Pickled Onions (see page 217; optional)*
- *Whisky Mac Hot Sauce (see page 218; optional)*

For the scones, score a shallow line around the circumference of each potato with a sharp knife and place in a large saucepan of salted cold water set over a high heat. Bring to the boil and cook until tender, then drain the potatoes and let them steam in the hot saucepan for 5 minutes before slipping off their skins. Watch your fingers as they will be steaming hot. Scatter 50g (1¾oz) flour onto your work surface and, using a potato ricer, rice the potatoes directly onto the flour. About halfway through the process, add the butter in thin slices to help it melt, then rice the remaining potatoes on top.

Once all the potatoes have been riced, add 1 teaspoon salt and another 50g (1¾oz) flour. Pull the mixture together with your hands, kneading gently and adding as much of the remaining flour as required to obtain a soft dough. You'll need to use a little intuition as the level of flour required will be dictated by the 'wetness' of your potatoes. Flour your worktop again, cut off a piece of the dough, then dust the top of it with a little more flour. Roll out to a rough circle, 5mm (¼ inch) thick (I use a circle cutter to make them neat). Repeat with the remaining dough.

Grease a frying pan very lightly with a piece of oiled kitchen paper and fry each scone on both sides until golden and blistered all over. Set aside.

Blitz all the filling ingredients in a food processor until well combined but not overworked. Spread each scone right to the edge with the filling, then cook, filling-side down, in a hot, oiled frying pan until golden. Flip each scone briefly to reheat on the other side.

For the slaw, mix the mustard, lemon juice, oil and a little salt together in a non-reactive bowl and toss through the cabbage, apple and chives.

Crumble some black pudding into a hot, oiled frying pan and cook until lightly crispy. Pile the black pudding and slaw onto your tacos. Top with my Gin-and-Tonic Pickled Onions, if you like, and some of my Whisky Mac Hot Sauce, if you like things spicy. Garnish with parsley leaves and some bird's eye chilli.

On the Side

6

The oldest and most traditional of Scottish cheeses, this is delicious in its simplicity. My mum recalls her Aunt Chrissie making crowdie in the Outer Hebrides as a child (they came from the Isle of Barra). Milk from the family cow would be left to sour naturally on the windowsill before being strained into curds and whey. Now, we'd be wary of doing that (and who has their own cow anyway?), so we use lemon juice to sour the milk before straining. The cheese can be used in the same way as cream cheese in all manner of sweet and savoury situations. The leftover whey can be reserved and is particularly good used in bread recipes, to replace the milk or water component.

Crowdie

Makes 1 small pot of cheese

- *1 litre (1¾ pints) good-quality whole milk*
- *3 tablespoons lemon juice*
- *½ teaspoon salt*

For black crowdie

- *3 teaspoons fine-ground oatmeal, toasted*
- *2 teaspoons ground black pepper*

Alternative option

- *2 teaspoons single cream*
- *1 teaspoon fine-ground oatmeal, toasted (optional)*
- *½ teaspoon ground black pepper (optional)*

To serve (optional)

- *Oatcakes*
- *Walnuts*
- *Dried apricots*
- *Thin apple slices*
- *Sultanas*

Place the milk in a saucepan and heat gently until you see small bubbles foaming at the edges. Remove from the heat and pour in the lemon juice. Using a spoon, gently agitate the mixture with up and down movements, then place back over a low heat if necessary until you see the curds separating. Remove from the heat, cover with a tea towel and leave for 30 minutes.

Place a double muslin into a sieve over a bowl and spoon the large curds gently into it with a slotted spoon until most have been separated. Pour the remaining whey and small curds through another muslin. Reserve the whey and transfer any curds into the other muslin. Sprinkle the salt over the curds and stir well. Tightly tie the muslin by the corners over the handle of a wooden spoon. Suspend it over the bowl and transfer to the refrigerator overnight (cover and chill the whey to use in other recipes).

The next day, tip the cheese into a bowl. In this state, you can roll it in toasted oatmeal and black pepper (this is called black crowdie). Alternatively, whisk in 2 teaspoons cream and transfer to a small pot. I like to sprinkle the top with toasted oatmeal and black pepper, but you can leave it plain, or flavour any way you like. Treat this as you would milk – it is generally good kept in the refrigerator for up to a week in an airtight container.

Enjoy with your choice of accompaniments.

Wild carrots were native to Scotland and consumed for centuries, but not the orange carrots we know today, which were only introduced in the late 16th century by Dutch and Flemish traders. Carrots form the base of many traditional Scottish dishes, from stews to mince and tatties, but they are a stunning vegetable when allowed to shine in their own right. This is a fabulous side dish for some lamb chops and crispy potatoes, but it can also hold centre stage with some good bread or even my Skillet Oatcake (see page 148) as a sharing dish.

Roasted Hot Honey Carrots on Creamed Crowdie

Serves 4

- *2 bunches of baby carrots, greens attached*
- *1–2 tablespoons olive oil*
- *½ teaspoon My Scottish 7-Spice Blend (see page 214)*
- *Generous drizzle of Whisky Hot Honey (see page 218), plus extra to serve*
- *Bread, to serve*

For the creamed crowdie

- *Crowdie (see page 110)*
- *2 tablespoons natural yogurt*
- *Small bunch of parsley*
- *Small bunch of chives*
- *½ teaspoon My Scottish 7-Spice Blend (see page 214)*
- *1 garlic clove, peeled*
- *Zest of 1 lemon*
- *Reserved whey or milk, to loosen (optional)*
- *Salt and ground black pepper*

For the carrot greens pesto

- *Greens from a bunch of carrots*
- *Small bunch of parsley*
- *Small bunch of chives*
- *100ml (3½fl oz) olive oil, plus extra if needed*
- *1 garlic clove, peeled*
- *Juice of ½ lemon*
- *Pinch of salt*

Preheat the oven to 180°C fan (400°F), Gas Mark 6.

Cut the green tops off the carrots (keep these to one side for a garnish), leaving a wee bit of green stalk. You can carefully peel the carrots, if you like, or just give them a scrub before placing in a roasting tin. Toss through the oil and 7-Spice Blend, then roast for about 30 minutes until starting to become golden. Remove from the oven and turn them. Squeeze over the hot honey, give the pan a good shake and return to the oven to caramelize for 5–10 minutes.

Meanwhile, put your crowdie into a food processor with the yogurt, herbs, 7-Spice Blend, garlic and lemon zest, and blitz it together. Add a little whey or milk to loosen to a spreading consistency, if you need to. Season to taste.

To make the carrot greens pesto, add everything to a blender and combine, adding a little extra oil, if required, to create a emulsion of drizzling consistency.

When you are ready to serve, spread the creamed crowdie on a plate and top with the caramelized roasted carrots, then drizzle over some Whisky Hot Honey and the carrot greens pesto. Sprinkle with a few fresh, frondy carrot greens and dig in, making sure to get in with some bread to mop up all that tasty crowdie.

Rumbledethumps is a traditional Scottish dish of mashed potatoes with onions and cabbage, topped with cheese and baked. The name comes from the sound it makes as the wooden spoon birls (an evocative Scottish word for 'spins' or 'twirls') around the sides of the pot. As Brussels sprouts are just wee cabbages, I love using them for this dish. It makes a fantastic Christmas side, but as cabbage and sprouts are interchangeable, you can be eating this all year round.

Rumbledethumps

Serves 4–6

- *1kg (2lb 4oz) potatoes, peeled and roughly chopped*
- *150ml (5fl oz) double cream*
- *75g (2¾oz) butter*
- *2 tablespoons olive oil*
- *2 small onions, finely sliced*
- *500g (1lb 2oz) Brussels sprouts, base trimmed and outer leaves removed, then finely sliced (use a food processor, if you have one)*
- *1 tablespoon Dijon mustard*
- *Large handful of chives, chopped*
- *Salt and ground black pepper*

For the topping

- *70g (2½oz) butter*
- *60g (2¼oz) fine-ground oatmeal*
- *40g (1½oz) panko breadcrumbs*
- *Leaves of 6 sprigs of thyme*
- *10 sage leaves, finely sliced*
- *Zest of 1 lemon*
- *90g (3¼oz) Cheddar cheese, grated*
- *Salt and ground black pepper*

Preheat the oven to 180°C fan (400°F), Gas Mark 6.

Place the potatoes in a large saucepan of salted cold water and bring to the boil. Cook until very tender, then drain and mash. Add 100ml (3½fl oz) of the cream, then beat with a wooden spoon and season to taste.

In a separate saucepan, melt the butter with the olive oil over a low heat, then add the onions and sprouts. Cover with the lid and soften, stirring occasionally, for about 20 minutes. When soft, remove the lid, turn the heat up and stir until slightly caramelized. Add to the mash, then 'rumbledethump' them together. Add the mustard, chives and remaining cream and season to taste. Set aside.

For the topping, melt the butter in a separate pan, then add all the other ingredients apart from the lemon zest and Cheddar. Toast over a medium heat until lightly golden, then add the zest and Cheddar. Season to taste and mix to combine.

Fill an ovenproof dish with your mash (I use a 23cm/9 inch round dish, 4cm/1½ inches deep), spreading it right to the edges. Cover evenly with the topping. Bake for 40 minutes until golden with a crunchy topping.

Serve with anything from roast chicken to steak, but feel free to let this shine as a vegetarian main meal served with a delicious salad.

Another Scottish name of wonderful Orcadian heritage for this delicious side dish. It's pretty simple really: neeps (swede) and tatties (potatoes) are cooked and mashed together. I prefer a slightly more potato-heavy ratio, but you can make it to your own taste. My daughter won't eat neeps on their own, but she loves this. Clearly, hidden veggies are the way to go. It's great with a traditional haggis but don't stop there – it works a treat with my Beef Olives (see page 104) and would be astounding with a simple roast chicken. You can also try the popular mash of carrots and neeps together – another amazing side dish.

Clapshot

Serves 4–6

- *900g (2lb) potatoes, peeled and roughly chopped*
- *600g (1lb 5oz) swede, peeled and roughly chopped (slightly smaller than the potatoes)*
- *50g (1¾oz) butter, plus extra to serve*
- *50g (1¾oz) beef dripping (optional)*
- *Bunch of chives, finely chopped*
- *Flaked salt and ground black pepper, to taste*

Place the potatoes and swede in a large saucepan of salted cold water and bring to the boil. Cook until tender to the point of a knife. Drain, add the butter and dripping (if using), season, then mash to your desired consistency.

Stir through most of the chopped chives and serve, seasoned with extra flaked salt and plenty of freshly ground black pepper. Finish with an extra knob of butter to melt over the top and a sprinkle of the remaining chives.

When I was growing up, we would often have oatmeal and butter on our boiled potatoes, particularly on Ayrshire Earlies. These days my family love a crushed roast potato, so I was inspired to make a roast version combined with skirlie (a traditional oatmeal side dish). I have added some rosemary and lemon, too, as they are the best friends of potatoes. Don't worry if you are vegetarian or vegan – you can easily substitute the beef dripping with any oil that you like.

Skirlie Roast Potatoes

Serves 4

- *1kg (2lb 4oz) baby potatoes*
- *Flaked salt, for sprinkling*
- *Olive oil, for drizzling*

For the skirlie coating

- *30g (1oz) fine-ground oatmeal*
- *3 sprigs of rosemary, leaves picked and finely chopped*
- *1–2 garlic cloves, crushed*
- *Zest of 1 lemon*
- *40ml (2½ tablespoons) beef dripping*
- *Pinch of salt*

Preheat the oven to 180°C fan (400°F), Gas Mark 6.

Place the potatoes in a large saucepan of salted cold water and bring to the boil. Cook until very tender. Drain, then let the potatoes steam in the hot pan for 5 minutes before transferring to a roasting tray and lightly crushing with a potato masher. Sprinkle with salt flakes, drizzle with olive oil and roast for about 40 minutes until lightly golden and starting to crisp up.

While the potatoes are cooking, make the skirlie coating. Place all the ingredients together in a small bowl, mix to combine, then set aside to firm up.

When the potatoes are ready, remove them from the oven (leaving it on). Carefully tear the potatoes in half by hand into a large bowl, crumble in your skirlie, add a drizzle of olive oil and mix thoroughly, ensuring the potatoes are well coated. Return the potatoes to the oven and cook for 15–20 minutes until lovely and crispy all over.

Serve the potatoes with a roast dinner or just have them as a delicious crispy snack to eat with a dip and drinks of choice. I like to pair them with a simple lemon mayonnaise and a martini.

Oatcakes have been eaten in Scotland for centuries and are incredibly simple to make. For these, I started with an inherited handwritten recipe (which specified self-raising flour) and have adapted it. Oatcakes have an austerity to them if eaten alone, but they add a perfect, textural crunch to a cheeseboard and are great with pâté. In some parts of Scotland, the locals won't eat stovies without one. You could also cut them into smaller discs and serve as canapés with Scottish-inspired toppings, or alongside a dip to nibble with drinks.

Oatcakes

Makes 15–16 oatcakes

- *20g (¾oz) dripping, pork fat, bacon fat or butter*
- *75ml (2½fl oz) boiling water*
- *125g (4½oz) oatmeal*
- *25g (scant 1oz) self-raising flour, plus extra for dusting*
- *½ teaspoon salt*

Preheat the oven to 180°C fan (400°F), Gas Mark 6.

Melt the fat in the measured boiling water.

Put all the dry ingredients in a bowl and add the water and fat mixture. Stir to combine, then tip out onto the work surface and knead together until all the oatmeal has been incorporated. Dust the work surface with flour, then dust the top of the dough. Roll out with a rolling pin, turning over and pressing in the edges to stop any cracking until it is about 3mm (⅛ inch) thick. Using a 6cm (2½ inch) round cutter, cut out 15–16 discs and place onto baking trays lined with greaseproof paper. You can reform the dough and roll it out again to get more out of it.

Bake for 15–20 minutes. The oatcakes should not brown all over – they should remain pale coloured, with a minimum amount of browning to any edges.

Leave to cool, then serve alongside anything you like!

This is the potato salad my mum always made, sometimes with the addition of a chopped hard-boiled egg – although the crispy skins are my addition. It's simple, delicious and perfect for any occasion. It's best eaten at room temperature just after it's been made. If there are any leftovers, roast them in the oven – it's almost worth making just to do that.

Mum's Potato Salad

Serves 4

- *12–15 small potatoes, skin on*
- *2 tablespoons natural yogurt*
- *2 tablespoons mayonnaise*
- *Squeeze of lemon juice*
- *4 tablespoons chopped soft herbs (I use chives and parsley)*
- *Neutral oil, for cooking the potato skins*
- *Seasonings for the potato skins (anything you like – try paprika, chilli powder, chicken seasoning or vinegar powder)*
- *Chopped chives, to garnish*
- *Gin-and-Tonic Pickled Onions (see page 217), to serve (optional)*
- *Salt and ground black pepper*

For the French dressing

- *2 tablespoons olive oil*
- *1 tablespoon red wine vinegar*
- *1 teaspoon Dijon mustard*
- *2 shallots, finely chopped*
- *Salt*

Score a shallow line around the circumference of each potato with a sharp knife. Place in a pan of salted cold water and bring to the boil. Simmer until perfectly tender. Cover with a tea towel and leave to steam in the hot pan for 5 minutes while you make the dressing.

In a large bowl, combine the olive oil, vinegar, mustard and shallots. Season with a little salt and mix well. Set aside.

Peel off the potato skins and set them aside, then chop the potatoes into chunks. While they are still warm, place them to the dressing and stir well to coat. Add the yogurt, mayo and lemon juice, and stir again. Add a massive grind of black pepper, then the herbs. Stir well and set aside.

Coat the reserved potato skins in a little oil, season with salt and pepper, then air fry at 180°C (350°F) or bake in a 180°C fan (400°F), Gas Mark 6 oven for 10–15 minutes until crispy, giving them a shoogle halfway through. Season with any spices or flavourings you like. I like vinegar powder, but you could use paprika, chilli powder or chicken seasoning.

Sprinkle the crispy potato skins over the potato salad, then garnish with a few chopped chives. Serve some of my Gin-and-Tonic Pickled Onions on the side, if you like.

Sweet Puddings

7

This sweet wonder was born through a combination of the classic Scottish teacake treat and a marshmallow tartlet in my gran's recipe book. Easy to make at home, the chocolate discs crack to reveal a soft marshmallow and jam filling, all enclosed in a chocolate pastry crust. It's as comfortable as a dessert as it is with a cup of tea.

'Teacake' Tarts

Makes 12 tarts

For the chocolate shortcrust pastry

- *200g (7oz) plain flour, plus extra for dusting*
- *50g (1¾oz) caster sugar*
- *20g (¾oz) cocoa powder*
- *Pinch of salt*
- *100g (3½oz) unsalted butter, plus extra for greasing*
- *1 egg*

For the chocolate discs

- *225g (8oz) chocolate (dark or milk)*
- *Freeze-dried raspberries, for sprinkling*

For the raspberry sauce

- *200g (7oz) raspberries*
- *100g (3½oz) caster sugar*
- *2 teaspoons raspberry jelly crystals*

For the marshmallow

- *3 egg whites*
- *150g (5½oz) caster sugar*
- *50g (1¾oz) glucose syrup*
- *½ teaspoon cream of tartar*
- *½ teaspoon vanilla paste*

For the pastry, add the flour, sugar, cocoa powder, salt and butter to a stand mixer fitted with a paddle attachment and mix until it resembles breadcrumbs. Add the egg and 1 tablespoon cold water and mix to combine. Press together using a little extra flour, then wrap in clingfilm and chill in the refrigerator for 15 minutes.

Preheat the oven to 180°C fan (400°F), Gas Mark 6. Grease the holes of a 12-cup muffin tin with butter.

Remove the pastry from the refrigerator and roll it to 3mm (⅛ inch) thick. Cut into discs, 9cm (3½ inches) in diameter, and place into the cups of the muffin tin. Line each with a muffin case and add a spoonful of baking beans or rice. Bake blind for 15 minutes, then remove the beans and cases and return to the oven for another 3 minutes. Leave the pastry cases to cool.

To make the chocolate discs, melt the chocolate and pour onto a sheet of greaseproof paper, using an offset spatula to spread it quite thinly (reserve a little of the chocolate for brushing). Sprinkle the chocolate sheet with freeze-dried raspberries and leave to set. Use the reserved melted chocolate to brush the insides of the cooled pastry cases.

When the chocolate sheet has set, warm a 5cm (2 inch) cookie cutter in boiling water and use it cut out 12 chocolate discs.

For the raspberry sauce, mash the raspberries in a saucepan with the sugar. Heat gently and simmer for 15 minutes. Mash again, then add the jelly crystals. Mix until well dissolved, then pass it all through a sieve to remove the seeds. Cover and leave to cool.

For the marshmallow filling, heat all the ingredients slowly in a heatproof bowl set over a pan of simmering water, stirring slowly until the sugar has dissolved, then beat on high with an electric hand whisk. Set a timer for 8 minutes, beating for that whole time, but take it off the heat after 6 minutes. Beat until it is VERY stiff. Place the mixture into a piping bag and cut the tip off when ready to assemble.

Pop some raspberry sauce into the base of each tart, then pipe in the marshmallow almost to the top. Finish with a chocolate disc.

Traditionally, a Tipsy Laird is the name given to a Scottish trifle, the main difference being that the sponge is soaked in a whisky-based drink as opposed to the 'English' way of soaking with sherry. My version goes another way, using Scottish spiced rum with ginger and mandarins, resulting in an alternative take on a classic dessert. Especially good at Christmas when mandarins are in season, it can be made as individual trifles or one big dish to share. This is best made several hours in advance, to allow the flavours to soak in.

Tipsy Laird

Makes 6–8 small trifles

For the gingerbread

- *250g (9oz) plain flour*
- *1 teaspoon ground ginger*
- *2 teaspoons My Scottish 5-Spice Blend (see page 214)*
- *100g (3½oz) unsalted butter*
- *2 tablespoons black treacle or molasses*
- *250ml (9fl oz) whole milk*
- *1 egg, beaten*
- *100g (3½oz) soft brown sugar*
- *1 teaspoon bicarbonate of soda*

For the rum and mandarin custard

- *3 egg yolks*
- *50g (1¾oz) caster sugar*
- *250ml (9fl oz) single cream*
- *50ml (2fl oz) whole milk*
- *1 teaspoon vanilla bean paste*
- *40g (1½oz) tapioca flour or cornflour*
- *25ml (1½ tablespoons) spiced rum*
- *Zest of 1 mandarin*
- *25g (scant 1oz) unsalted butter*

For the ginger meringues

- *3 egg whites*
- *140g (5oz) caster sugar*
- *¼ teaspoon cream of tartar*
- *1 teaspoon ground ginger*
- *Orange food colouring (optional)*

For the gingerbread, preheat the oven to 160°C fan (350°F), Gas Mark 4. Line a 20 × 28cm (8 × 11 inch) deep-sided baking tin with nonstick baking paper.

Sift the flour and spices into a bowl. In a small pan, melt the butter and treacle or molasses together, then add to the flour mixture. In the same pan, gently warm the milk, then add to the mixture with the egg, sugar and bicarbonate of soda. Mix well and pour into the prepared tin. Bake for 25 minutes or until an inserted skewer comes out clean. Leave to cool in the tin.

For the custard, beat the egg yolks and sugar until pale and fluffy. Meanwhile, gently warm the cream, milk and vanilla bean paste in a small pan. Beat the tapioca flour or cornflour into the egg mixture, then gradually add the warmed cream and milk, beating to combine. Pour in the rum, then transfer back to the pan. Stir over a gentle heat until thickened, then add the mandarin zest and butter. Turn off the heat and whisk until the butter has melted and is combined, then chill in the refrigerator until ready to use.

For the meringues, in the very clean bowl of a stand mixer, beat the egg whites until frothy, then gradually add the sugar, beating all the time. Add the cream of tartar and ginger and beat till glossy. Alternatively, use a hand whisk but do make sure your mixing bowl is very clean. Transfer to a piping bag (you can paint stripes on the inside with orange food colour, if you like), then pipe small kisses onto a baking sheet lined with nonstick baking paper. Bake in a preheated oven, 100°C fan (250°F) Gas Mark ½, for 30–40 minutes until the meringues lift off the paper easily. Turn the oven off and leave them inside with the door ajar until fully cooled.

For the fruit and soaking liquid

- *8 mandarins*
- *60ml (4 tablespoons) spiced rum*
- *3 heaped tablespoons orange marmalade*

For the cream

- *300ml (10fl oz) whipping cream*
- *4 teaspoons spiced rum*
- *Zest of 1 mandarin, plus extra to garnish*
- *2 tablespoons icing sugar*

Peel the mandarins with a knife, cutting of the peel and the pith, then carefully segment the fruit over a bowl, cutting the flesh out from inside the membranes, and reserving the juice. Strain the juice from the fruit.

For the soaking liquid, pour the juice into a bowl, add the spiced rum and marmalade and stir well.

To make the cream, beat all the ingredients together until thick and transfer to a piping bag.

I like to layer these trifles individually in jars (see photograph overleaf). To assemble, cut out a disc of gingerbread, about 5cm (2 inches) in diameter, and place in the bottom of a jar. Drizzle over some of the soaking liquid. Spoon in a layer of custard, then add some mandarin segments. Top with half a disc of gingerbread and more of the soaking liquid, then add a dollop of cream and a ginger meringue. Garnish with extra mandarin zest. These can sit in the refrigerator for 24 hours to let the flavours develop before serving, if required.

A 'deep-fried Mars Bar' is the stuff of Scottish legend. It must have started as an urban myth about Scottish folk deep-frying everything; it certainly was not a 'thing' when I was growing up. It does intrigue me though, so I set out to make a version that turns it into a dinner party showstopper. With whisky salted caramel, malted milk ice cream, dark chocolate mousse for a touch of bitterness and the crunch of a light batter heavily scented with Scottish spices and sugar, it's decadent, full of flavour and with a hint of sophistication.

Deconstructed 'Deep-Fried Mars Bar'

Serves 8

For the malted milk ice cream

- *30g (1oz) full cream milk powder*
- *700ml (1¼ pints) whole milk*
- *50g (1¾oz) caster sugar*
- *½ teaspoon powdered gelatine*
- *30g (1oz) malted milk powder (such as Horlicks)*
- *1 teaspoon good cocoa powder*
- *125ml (4fl oz) sweetened condensed milk*
- *30g (1oz) glucose*

For the chocolate mousse

- *100g (3½oz) dark chocolate (70% cocoa solids)*
- *100g (3½oz) milk chocolate*
- *100ml (3½fl oz) hot water*
- *3 eggs, separated*
- *30g (1oz) caster sugar*

For the ice cream, toast the full cream milk powder in a dry pan until golden all over and with a lightly toasty caramel fragrance. Remove to a bowl.

Place the milk and sugar in a saucepan and heat until small bubbles form at the edges of the pan. While the milk is heating, put the gelatine into 1 tablespoon cold water to soften.

Whisk the toasted milk powder into the hot milk along with the malted milk powder and cocoa, then add the sweetened condensed milk and glucose, followed by the softened gelatine. Heat through until well combined, then strain through a very fine sieve into a bowl. Cover and refrigerate until the mixture is cold, then churn in an ice-cream machine according to the manufacturer's instructions. This can be stored in the freezer until ready to use.

For the chocolate mousse, melt both chocolates and the measured hot water together in a heatproof bowl set above a pan of simmering water, stirring until glossy. Sit the bowl in a larger bowl filled with cold water and ice and beat with electric beaters to cool it a little before beating in the egg yolks until well combined. Remove from the water bath. In a separate, spotlessly clean bowl, beat the egg whites to soft peaks, then gradually add the sugar, beating until the mixture is stiff and glossy. Spoonful by spoonful, add it to the chocolate mix and gently fold through, cutting and folding with a metal spoon so as not to lose the air. When it is all combined, transfer to a bowl or tub, cover and refrigerate until set.

For the whisky salted caramel

- *200g (7oz) caster sugar*
- *100ml (3½fl oz) single cream*
- *4 teaspoons whisky*
- *20g (¾oz) unsalted butter*
- *½ teaspoon smoked salt flakes*

For the spiced sugar dust

- *2 tablespoons caster sugar*
- *1 teaspoon My Scottish 5-Spice Blend (see page 214)*
- *¼ teaspoon salt*

For the crispy batter bits

- *40g (1½oz) plain flour*
- *30g (1oz) cornflour*
- *½ teaspoon baking powder*
- *Pinch of salt*
- *75ml (2½fl oz) cold water*
- *1 teaspoon malt vinegar*
- *Vegetable oil, for deep-frying*

For the whisky salted caramel, heat the sugar gently in a pan until it has dissolved and turned a rich caramel colour. Add the cream and whisky and stir until all lumps are dissolved. Stir through the butter. If you need to, you can sieve it at this point to get rid of any stubborn sugary lumps. Pour into a bowl to cool, then stir through the smoked salt. Decant into a squeezy bottle.

For the spiced sugar dust, combine all the ingredients in a bowl and set aside.

For the crispy batter bits, heat enough oil in a deep, heavy-based pan or a deep-fat fryer to 180°C (350°F), or until a cube of bread browns in 30 seconds.

Sift the flours, baking powder and salt into a bowl, then gradually whisk in the measured cold water until smooth. Add the vinegar and combine. Dip your fingers into the batter and drizzle it from a height into the hot oil. It will form small droplets. Fry until crispy, then remove with a slotted spoon to drain on kitchen paper. While the bits are still warm, toss them in the spiced sugar dust.

When ready to serve, spoon the chocolate mousse onto a plate. Make an indent in the middle, then put a scoop of the malted milk ice cream on top. Drizzle the whisky salted caramel over and finish with the crispy batter bits (see photograph on previous page).

This is not a traditional Scottish recipe, rather a combination of two of my mum's favourite showstopping desserts that hold a lot of nostalgic memories for me. One was a Gâteau Diane, a Cordon Bleu recipe of layered meringue and chocolate cream. The other was a hazelnut cake, decorated with hazelnuts dipped in caramel, something I always marvelled at as a child. This cake is a showstopper in its own right, with the chocolate and hazelnuts working their magic together to create new memories.

Gâteau Marion

Serves 12

For the meringues

- *6 egg whites*
- *300g (10½oz) caster sugar*
- *150g (5½oz) skinned hazelnuts, finely ground*
- *1 teaspoon My Scottish 5-Spice Blend (see page 214)*

For the caramel hazelnuts

- *100g (3½oz) caster sugar*
- *10 hazelnuts*

For the filling

- *200ml (7fl oz) whipping cream*
- *400g (14oz) chocolate (half dark, half milk), melted*
- *800ml (1⅓ pints) soured cream*

For the topping

- *1 × 30g (1oz) milk chocolate flake bar*
- *100g (3½oz) bar of dark chocolate*

Add the egg whites to the very clean bowl of a stand mixer and beat to soft peaks. With the whisk running, slowly add the sugar, little by little, letting it fully incorporate before you add more. Alternatively, you can use a hand whisk but do make sure your mixing bowl is very clean. When the meringue is beautifully stiff and glossy, fold through the ground hazelnuts and 5-Spice Blend.

On four baking trays, mark out circles about 20cm (8 inches) in diameter and divide the meringue among them. Using a palette knife, smooth the meringue into circle shapes. Pop into a preheated oven, 120°C fan (275°F), Gas Mark 1, for 1 hour, then turn the oven off and leave the meringues inside overnight, if possible. The meringues can be stored in an airtight container until you are ready to use them.

To make the caramel hazelnuts, put the sugar and 1 tablespoon water into a small pan and bring to a simmer. Let it bubble away to a mid-amber colour, then remove it from the heat. Poke a wooden skewer into the side of each hazelnut. Lay some greaseproof paper on the floor, as this can get messy. I also place a heavy baking tray on the edge of the worktop to hold each skewer in place. Dip a nut into the caramel, making sure it is well covered (you know the caramel is ready when it sticks well and does not fall off). Twist it around, then place one end of the skewer under the baking tray and let the caramel drip to the floor. Do that with all the hazelnuts and let them set.

Beat the whipping cream for the filling to soft peaks. In a separate bowl, beat the melted chocolate into the soured cream. When it's well combined and thickened, fold through the whipped cream.

Now it's time to build your gâteau. Divide the cream among the meringues, spreading it out to the edges. With the help of a fish slice, carefully layer the meringue circles on top of one another. Break the chocolate flake up into a bowl. Use a potato peeler to shave some of the dark chocolate into it. Scatter the chocolate shards all over the top layer of meringue, then arrange the caramel hazelnuts around the edge of the circle. Stunning!

Steamed sponge: comforting, nostalgic and delicious. It's somehow seen as old fashioned. I can tell you that this recipe is all those things, but it's also more than happy in a modern-day setting. A total delight to eat – light, fragrant and delicious – it's the pure simplicity that I love. This is a must-try recipe and a doddle to make. It's a real pleasure to see eyes light up after that first mouthful – a definite WOW!

Steamed Ginger Sponge

Makes 4 individual puddings

- *100g (3½oz) unsalted butter, softened, plus extra for greasing*
- *100g (3½oz) soft brown sugar*
- *1 teaspoon baking powder*
- *2 eggs*
- *100g (3½oz) plain flour*
- *1 teaspoon My Scottish 5-Spice Blend (see page 214)*
- *1 teaspoon ground ginger*
- *Zest and juice of 1 lemon*
- *100ml (3½fl oz) golden syrup*
- *100ml (3½fl oz) ginger syrup (you can use the syrup from a jar of crystallized ginger)*

For the custard

- *3 egg yolks*
- *50g (1¾oz) caster sugar*
- *250ml (9fl oz) single cream*
- *50ml (2fl oz) whole milk*
- *1 teaspoon vanilla bean paste*
- *40g (1½oz) tapioca flour or cornflour*
- *30g (1oz) unsalted butter*

In a large bowl, beat the butter and sugar together until light and creamy. Add the baking powder, one of the eggs and half the flour, beat well, then add the other egg, the rest of the flour, the spices and beat well. Add the lemon zest and mix thoroughly. Set aside while you make the syrup.

Measure the golden syrup and ginger syrup into a jug and warm slightly in the microwave (you could also do this in a pan over a low heat). Add the lemon juice and whisk into the warmed syrup.

Preheat the oven to 180°C fan (400°F), Gas Mark 6.

Butter the inside of four dariole moulds (mine are 7.5cm/3 inches in diameter, 5cm/2 inches high, 165ml/5½fl oz in capacity), then pour in the syrup to a height of about 5mm (¼ inch). Divide the sponge mixture between the moulds, then place into a small roasting tray. Pour in a kettle full of boiling water to about half the height of the moulds, then cover the whole thing loosely in kitchen foil.

Bake for 40–45 minutes, or until an inserted skewer comes out clean.

For the custard, beat the egg yolks and sugar until pale and fluffy. Meanwhile, gently warm the cream, milk and vanilla bean paste in a small pan. Beat the tapioca flour or cornflour into the egg mixture, then gradually add the warmed cream and milk, beating to combine. Transfer back to the pan and stir over a gentle heat until thickened. Turn off the heat and whisk in the butter until combined.

Remove the sponges from the water bath and carefully loosen the tops with a knife, then tip onto individual plates. Warm the syrup again slightly and pour over the top of the sponges. Back that up with a hefty pour of custard, then tuck in and savour. It's mind-blowing stuff, I promise.

Cranachan is probably the best-known traditional Scottish dessert. Scottish flavours run through each element of this version, from the toasted oat crumble and no-churn whisky caramel-swirl oat ice cream to the Drambuie-macerated raspberries and whisky oat snaps. There are a few simple steps, but the magic happens when it all comes together.

My Cranachan

Serves 6

For the toasted oat cream

- *50g (1¾oz) porridge oats*
- *500ml (18fl oz) whipping cream*
- *1 teaspoon vanilla bean paste*

For the honey toasted oats

- *50g (1¾oz) honey*
- *50g (1¾oz) unsalted butter*
- *100g (3½oz) porridge oats*
- *Pinch of salt*

For the whisky oat snaps

- *50g (1¾oz) honey*
- *50g (1¾oz) butter*
- *50g (1¾oz) brown sugar*
- *75g (2⅔oz) oat flour*
- *1 teaspoon whisky*

For the oat condensed milk

- *50g (1¾oz) porridge oats*
- *700ml (1¼ pints) water*
- *200g (7oz) caster sugar*
- *Pinch of salt*

For the whisky caramel

- *100g (3½oz) honey*
- *25g (scant 1oz) unsalted butter*
- *1 tablespoon whisky*
- *100ml (3½fl oz) single cream*

For the macerated raspberries

- *50ml (2fl oz) Drambuie*
- *240g (8½oz) raspberries*

To serve

- *Icing sugar, for dusting*
- *Wee dram of whisky (optional)*

Preheat the oven to 180°C fan (400°F), Gas Mark 6. Start with the toasted oat cream. Spread the oats across a baking tray and toast for 20 minutes until golden. While the oats are still hot, transfer to a small bowl and add the cream and vanilla bean paste. Mix well, cover and leave to steep overnight in the refrigerator.

For the honey toasted oats, melt the honey and butter in a small saucepan over a low heat, then mix together with the oats and salt. Spread the mixture across a baking tray and bake for 15 minutes until golden. Allow to cool, then break up and set aside.

For the oat snaps, line two baking trays with nonstick baking paper. Melt the honey and butter, then stir through the other ingredients. Drop teaspoon-sized amounts of the mixture onto the lined trays, spacing them well apart. Bake for about 10 minutes until golden.

To make the oat condensed milk, add the oats and measured water to a blender and blend for 30 seconds to obtain a creamy, white liquid. Strain twice through a muslin set over a large bowl. Pour this milk into a small saucepan set over a low heat, add the sugar and salt and cook, stirring, until thickened. Remove from the heat and set aside to cool.

For the whisky caramel, melt the honey and butter together in a small saucepan over a low heat and allow to simmer until the mixture thickens and darkens in colour. Add the whisky and cream and continue to simmer until you have a thick, glossy caramel.

For my no-churn ice cream, strain 350ml (12fl oz) of the toasted oat cream with 350ml (12fl oz) of the oat condensed milk into a stand mixer and beat until thick. Transfer half the mixture to a plastic tub, add about a third of the whisky honey caramel and swirl through with a skewer. Add the rest of the cream mixture and another third of the caramel and swirl again. Freeze.

For the macerated raspberries, warm the Drambuie and half the berries in a saucepan over a medium heat. Mash together with the back of a spoon until syrupy, then allow to cool. Mix through the remaining raspberries.

To assemble, let the ice cream soften for 20 minutes, then layer the dessert on plates, starting with the honey toasted oats, then a scoop of ice cream, a drizzle of the remaining whisky caramel, the raspberries and then a whisky oat snap. Dust with icing sugar and serve with a dram on the side, if you like.

A clootie dumpling is a traditional Scottish fruit cake. The name is derived from the 'cloot' (linen cloth) that the dumpling is cooked in. It's often likened to Christmas cake, but it's lighter and can be eaten warm with custard, cold with butter and jam, or fried up with your Scottish breakfast. I like to serve mine for breakfast, fried with streaky bacon, berries and a maple syrup butter and sprinkled with smoked salt flakes – sensational!

Clootie Dumpling

Serves 12

- *300g (10½oz) self-raising flour, plus extra for dusting*
- *100g (3½oz) suet (beef or vegetable)*
- *100g (3½oz) brown sugar*
- *100g (3½oz) breadcrumbs*
- *3 teaspoons My Scottish 5-Spice Blend (see page 214)*
- *1 teaspoon flaked salt*
- *100g (3½oz) currants*
- *100g (3½oz) sultanas*
- *100g (3½oz) pitted dates, chopped*
- *1 apple, grated*
- *2 eggs, beaten*
- *2 tablespoons black treacle*
- *Splash of whole milk*
- *Warm custard, to serve*

In a large bowl, mix together all the dry ingredients and dried fruit, then add the grated apple, eggs, treacle and a splash of milk. Mix together, adding more milk when necessary to make a sticky, stiff dough.

I use a muslin for this, as the square shape works better than a tea towel. Lay the cloth in the sink and pour over boiling water. Move it to your work surface, dust well with flour, then place your dough in the middle. Gather the cloth up to make a loose parcel and tie securely with kitchen string. Your dumpling needs room to expand so don't wrap it too tightly. Put a plate or a trivet in the bottom of a large saucepan, place the clootie dumpling on top and almost cover with boiling water. Bring to a simmer, cover and cook over a low heat for 3½ hours. Keep checking and top up the water when necessary.

Close to the end, preheat the oven to 170°C fan (375°F), Gas Mark 5.

Carefully lift the dumpling out, remove the muslin and place on a nonstick baking tray. Bake for 10–15 minutes until you can see a skin has formed.

Serve straight away with custard or cool and slice for the next day.

Shake things up at Christmas and make this Scottish twist on a mince pie. Actually, make it all year round – it's totally delicious. Traditionally, this is a dense fruit tart, but I have modernized it, making a light frangipane from the walnuts and using that as a holding device for the fruit, all encased in a walnut and whisky shortcrust pastry. It works so well, and although there are distinct mince pie vibes, this tart is delicious in its own right.

Ecclefechan Tart

Serves 10–12

For the sweet shortcrust pastry

- *200g (7oz) plain flour*
- *50g (1¾oz) walnuts, ground to a flour*
- *1 tablespoon caster sugar*
- *Pinch of salt*
- *125g (4½oz) unsalted butter, plus extra for greasing*
- *1 tablespoon whisky*

For the filling

- *2 tablespoons lemon juice*
- *1 tablespoon whisky*
- *150g (5½oz) currants*
- *50g (1¾oz) sultanas*
- *50g (1¾oz) dried cranberries*
- *50g (1¾oz) glacé cherries, chopped*
- *125g (4½oz) unsalted butter*
- *125g (4½oz) soft brown sugar*
- *2 eggs*
- *25g (scant 1oz) plain flour*
- *100g (3½oz) ground walnuts*
- *1 teaspoon ground cinnamon*
- *½ teaspoon salt*
- *Zest of 1 lemon, plus extra to garnish*

To serve

- *Icing sugar*
- *Crème fraîche*

In a stand mixer fitted with the paddle attachment, mix the flour, ground walnuts, sugar, salt and butter until the mixture resembles breadcrumbs. Add the whisky and 1 tablespoon cold water and mix until it all comes together. Remove from the mixer, form into a thick disc, cover with clingfilm and refrigerate for 30 minutes.

Preheat the oven to 180°C fan (400°F), Gas Mark 6. Grease a 25cm (10 inch) tart tin with butter.

Remove the pastry dough from the refrigerator and roll out thinly until it's large enough to fit the tin. Carefully lift the pastry over the tin and gently press the pastry into the edges. Trim the edges with a knife. Fill with crumpled nonstick baking paper and baking beans or rice and bake blind for 10 minutes, then remove the paper and beans and cook for a further 6 minutes. Leave to cool.

For the filling, warm the lemon juice and whisky in a small pan, then stir through the currants, sultanas, cranberries and cherries. Set aside for 1 hour.

In a large bowl, beat the butter and sugar until creamy, then beat in the eggs with the flour until well incorporated. Stir through the ground walnuts, cinnamon, salt, lemon zest and soaked fruit.

Fill the tart case with the filling and use a palette knife to smooth it to the edges. Bake for 35 minutes.

Leave to cool, then remove from the tin, dust with icing sugar and serve with crème fraîche garnished with lemon zest.

Could this be the best dessert of all time? It's certainly one of my favourites – it's my Achilles heel if I see this on a menu. Easy to make at home, here it's made in a larger dish and cut into portions. Serve it with ice cream or custard, it's up to you.

Sticky Toffee Pudding

Serves 6–8

- *200g (7oz) pitted dates*
- *175ml (6fl oz) boiling water*
- *80g (2¾oz) unsalted butter, softened, plus extra for greasing*
- *2 tablespoons black treacle*
- *50g (1¾oz) soft brown sugar*
- *2 eggs*
- *2 teaspoons baking powder*
- *1 teaspoon bicarbonate of soda*
- *160g (5¾oz) plain flour*
- *1 teaspoon vanilla extract*
- *100ml (3½fl oz) whole milk*
- *Vanilla ice cream, to serve*

For the sauce

- *150g (5½oz) soft brown sugar*
- *100g (3½oz) unsalted butter*
- *200ml (7fl oz) single cream*
- *1 tablespoon black treacle*
- *¼ teaspoon smoked flaked salt*

Put the dates in a bowl and pour the measured boiling water over them. Leave to soften for at least 15 minutes, then blend to a purée.

In a large bowl, cream together the butter and treacle, then add the sugar and continue to mix. Beat one egg in at a time, then add the baking powder, bicarbonate of soda, flour, vanilla extract and milk and beat until well combined. Fold through the puréed date mixture.

Preheat the oven to 180°C fan (400°F), Gas Mark 6. Butter and line a 20 × 26cm (8 × 10½ inch) baking dish.

Pour the batter into the prepared dish and give it a tap to level it out. Bake for 20–25 minutes, or until an inserted skewer comes out clean.

Meanwhile, make the sauce. Combine the sugar, butter, cream and treacle in a saucepan and gently bring to a simmer. Cook for 10 minutes, then add the smoked flaked salt and stir through.

When the pudding is baked, poke a few holes across the top and pour a little sauce over. Cut into squares and serve with a little more sauce poured over, then add a scoop of vanilla ice cream, then serve any remaining sauce on the side.

Your Daily Bread

8

This is a cross between a bannock (see page 155 for my recipe), an oatcake and a pancake. Inspired by socca, the flatbread from the South of France made with chickpea flour, I thought this could work with oat flour. It's very easy to make in a hot grill oven, and if you have a pizza oven, it's perfect in there, too. Great on the side of just about anything, it makes a lovely alternative to bread. It's delicious served with my Confit Sardines (see page 59).

Skillet Oatcake

Serves 4–6

- *100g (3½oz) rolled oats*
- *250ml (9fl oz) water*
- *2 tablespoons olive oil, plus extra for cooking and serving*
- *½ teaspoon salt*
- *Pinch of My Scottish 7-Spice Blend (see page 214)*
- *Pinch of flaked sea salt*

In a food processor, blitz your oats to a flour, then tip into a bowl and add the measured water, oil and salt. Stir well, cover and let it sit for 1–2 hours, no more.

When you are ready to cook, preheat an oven on the grill setting to 240°C (475°F) and place a cast-iron skillet in there to get really hot.

Carefully remove the skillet from the oven and pour enough oil in to swirl around the base and sides. Pour the oat batter in and swirl it to the edges, like a big pancake (you can use a spatula or spoon to help do this). Get it straight back into the oven. It will take around 10–15 minutes to cook – but keep an eye on it. It's ready when it's crispy all round the edges and blistered with colour over the surface.

Take it out and carefully remove to a wooden board or large plate. Sprinkle a pinch each of 7-Spice Blend and flaked salt over the top and drizzle with more olive oil. Cut up and enjoy.

Using oats in bread is a tradition long held in Scotland. Hydrating those oats by making porridge traps moisture in the dough, resulting in a chewy, bubbly texture, a delicious flavour and nutritional benefits. The dough is incredibly adaptable and I have included three different ways to bake it.

Porridge Bread Dough

Serves 10–12

For the porridge

- *50g (1¾oz) fine-ground oatmeal*
- *300ml (10fl oz) water*
- *4 teaspoons olive oil, plus extra for greasing*
- *2 teaspoons honey*

For the dough

- *450g (1lb) strong white bread flour, plus extra for dusting*
- *10g (¼oz) salt*
- *7g packet of fast-action dried yeast*
- *250ml (9fl oz) water*

First, make the porridge. Combine the oats and measured water in a pan and bring to a simmer, stirring. Let it simmer for 5 minutes or so until it is thickened and smooth. Stir through the olive oil and honey. Remove to a bowl until it cools a little, covering the surface with a piece of clingfilm to stop a skin forming.

To make the dough, combine the flour and salt in a large bowl, then add the porridge and stir until it resembles breadcrumbs. Add the yeast and water and mix thoroughly with a spatula. Cover and leave for 15 minutes.

Then, with a wet hand, grab the edge of the dough, stretch up and place on the top. Do this on all four corners of the dough, then flip the whole thing over. Cover for 15 minutes, then repeat. Do this another two to three times – you should see the tension in the dough increasing every time.

Once your dough is mixed and stretched, oil another large bowl and put the dough in, flipping until it's covered in the oil. Leave it to double in size, then cover and leave in the refrigerator overnight. The next day, you will be met with a jiggly, bubbly dough.

Baking variations

Porridge Focaccia (opposite)

Additional ingredients

- *2 tablespoons olive oil, plus extra for drizzling*
- *1 tablespoon fine-ground oatmeal*
- *1 teaspoon flaked salt*
- *Bone Marrow Butter (see page 53), to serve (optional)*

Tip the dough out onto an oiled and lined baking tray. Using oiled fingers, fold the two sides into the middle, then flip. Gently ease it out to a rectangle and leave until the dough has doubled in size and is filling the tray. Drizzle with more olive oil, sprinkle with fine-ground oatmeal, dimple all over with your fingers, then sprinkle with flaked salt. Give it a shoogle – so satisfying! Get into a preheated oven, 200°C fan (425°F), Gas Mark 7, for 25–30 minutes. Remove to a rack to cool, then slice and enjoy. It makes the BEST sandwiches, epic toast, and is great with the Bone Marrow Butter from my Potted Hough.

For the confit garlic
- *2 garlic bulbs, cloves separated and peeled*
- *1 sprig of rosemary*
- *2 sprigs of thyme*
- *Olive oil, to cover*

For the garlic butter
- *250g (9oz) unsalted butter*
- *10 confit garlic cloves (see above)*
- *1 tablespoon My Scottish 7-Spice Blend (see page 214)*
- *1 teaspoon My Scottish 7-Spice Salt (see page 214)*
- *1 tablespoon garlic oil (from the garlic confit, see above)*

For filling and topping
- *120g (4oz) mozzarella cheese, grated*
- *120g (4oz) peppercorn Cheddar cheese, grated*
- *50g (1¾oz) Parmesan cheese, grated*
- *3 thyme sprigs, leaves only*

Porridge Tear-and-Share Garlic Bread (above)

First, make the garlic confit. Place the garlic cloves, rosemary and thyme in a small saucepan and cover with olive oil. Bring to a simmer and leave on as low a heat as possible for about 30 minutes until the cloves are very soft. Decant into a jar.

To make the garlic butter, blend all the ingredients together and chill in the refrigerator.

Tip the dough out onto a floured work surface and divide into 12 equal pieces. Press them out into rectangles and add a teaspoon of garlic butter into each one, followed by a good pinch of grated cheese – I use grated mozzarella and peppercorn Cheddar (keep some to sprinkle on later). Fold in the dough around the cheese to seal, turn over and roll into balls on your work surface using the palm of your hand.

Generously butter a baking tray or dish (I use a 30cm/12 inch circular, nonstick dish) with a little more garlic butter, then cover in a layer of grated Parmesan for a cheesy crust (again, keep some to sprinkle on later). Place the dough balls into the dish and leave to double in size. Meanwhile, preheat the oven to 220°C (475°F), Gas Mark 9.

Bake for 15 minutes until golden and almost cooked.

Remove from the oven and brush all over with more garlic butter (you will have some left over), then top with another sprinkling of your cheeses. Put back into the oven for a final 5 minutes or so until they are golden and bubbling. Sprinkle a few fresh thyme leaves over the top, then take to the table and let your guests pull apart and enjoy!

Porridge Dinner Rolls (below)

Tip the dough out onto a floured work surface. Divide it into 12 pieces (I use weighing scales to ensure they are equal in size). Fold the edges of each ball into the middle and pinch it together, turn it over and use the palm of your hand to roll it into a ball on the work surface. Place into a floured baking tray (mine is 23 × 30 × 5cm/9 × 12 × 2 inches). Fit all the rolls in, dust with extra flour, then cover and leave to double in size. Bake in a preheated oven, 220°C (475°F), Gas Mark 9, for 15 minutes.

This is a quick and easy traditional Scottish bread, not unlike a big scone. It is a non-yeasted bread that uses plain flour combined with fine-ground oatmeal and raising agents to leaven it. It's one of those brilliant breads you can eat with soup or with breakfast, that's delicious warm from the oven and it's on the table from start to finish in just over 30 minutes. I like to serve mine with cream cheese, Scottish smoked salmon and chives.

Scottish Soda Bread (Fife Bannock)

Serves 4

- *150ml (5fl oz) whole milk*
- *1 tablespoon vinegar (malt or white)*
- *175g (6oz) plain flour, plus extra for dusting*
- *½ teaspoon bicarbonate of soda*
- *1 teaspoon cream of tartar*
- *125g (4½oz) fine-ground oatmeal*
- *½ teaspoon caster sugar*
- *½ teaspoon salt*
- *30g (1oz) lard (or unsalted butter)*

Preheat the oven to 180°C fan (400°F), Gas Mark 6.

Mix the milk with the vinegar, stir and leave to the side to thicken slightly. This makes a homemade buttermilk. You can use shop-bought buttermilk, but I find that this is a bread that you want to be able to make on a whim with what you have in the house – and who has buttermilk in the refrigerator every day?

Sift the flour, bicarbonate of soda and cream of tartar into a bowl, then add the oatmeal, sugar and salt and stir through. Add the lard and rub it in until the mixture resembles breadcrumbs. Add your buttermilk, then stir briefly to combine. Tip out onto a well-floured work surface and bring the dough gently together with your hands into a round. Pop it onto a lined baking tray and mark a cross on the top.

Bake for about 25 minutes. This is best served warm and freshly made.

Note: Feel free to add cheese, herbs or nuts to the dough at the mixing stage to change up the flavour profile.

There are two types of bread used in the common Scottish vernacular: plain and pan. Plain loaves are a commercially baked batch bread unique to Scotland. They only have a crust on the top and bottom, as the loaves are baked touching each other in large trays. They have a well-fired crust and a tall shape, and are traditionally wrapped in a tartan-print waxed paper. Pan loaf, obviously baked in a pan or tin, has a crust all the way round. It's a great sandwich bread and, of the two, is the one that's achievable in a home oven. You will need two lidded 19 × 11 × 10cm (7½ × 4½ × 4 inch) Pullman loaf tins for this recipe.

Pan Loaf

Makes 2 loaves

- *10g (¼oz) fast-action dried yeast*
- *15g (½oz) caster sugar*
- *300ml (10fl oz) water at room temperature (NOT lukewarm)*
- *750g (1lb 10oz) strong white bread flour*
- *15g (½oz) salt*
- *90g (3¼oz) unsalted butter, melted, plus extra, at room temperature, to serve*
- *150ml (5fl oz) whole milk*
- *Oil, for greasing*

Add the yeast and 1 teaspoon of the sugar to the measured water, stir and set aside for 15 minutes to activate.

Add the flour, salt and the remaining sugar to the bowl of a stand mixer and combine. Add the melted butter to the milk. When the yeast has bloomed, pour the mixture along with the butter and milk mixture into the flour and mix well. Continue mixing for around 10 minutes until you have a smooth dough. Remove to an oiled bowl, cover with a tea towel and allow to double in size – this will take about 1 hour.

Tip the dough onto a floured work surface and divide into two balls that are approximately 650g (1lb 7oz) each. Flatten them out slightly, then fold as you would a letter, folding the top third in and bringing the bottom third up to cover it. Give it a 90-degree turn, then roll up into a rectangle. Oil your two Pullman loaf tins, then place your dough rectangles inside, seam-side down. Pop the lids on and leave until they've risen almost to the lid.

Meanwhile, preheat the oven to 200°C fan (425°F), Gas Mark 7.

Bake the loaves for 30 minutes. The internal temperature of the loaves should be around or slightly over 93°C (199°F) when they are cooked properly, and if you are concerned you can check this with a digital food thermometer.

Remove from the oven, then tip the bread immediately out of the tins onto a wire rack. Let them cool a little before slicing and serving with butter.

These are a beloved part of a Scottish breakfast and were a regular on our family weekend breakfast menu when I was growing up. They are easy to make at home. You can prepare the dough the night before so they are ready to rise and cook fresh for breakfast the next morning.

Morning Rolls

Makes 9 rolls

- *12g (⅓oz) caster sugar*
- *7g packet of fast-action dried yeast*
- *400ml (14fl oz) water at room temperature (NOT lukewarm)*
- *600g (1lb 5oz) strong white bread flour, plus extra for dusting*
- *12g (⅓oz) salt*
- *40g (1½oz) lard*
- *Oil, for greasing*
- *Semolina or rice flour, for dusting*

Stir 1 teaspoon of the sugar and all of the yeast into the measured water and leave for 15 minutes to activate.

Meanwhile, in a large bowl, combine the remaining sugar with the flour and salt. Add the lard and rub in with your fingertips until the mixture resembles breadcrumbs.

Combine the flour mixture and yeast mixture in a stand mixer fitted with a dough hook and knead until the dough is smooth and elastic. Tip into an oiled plastic tub, cover with clingfilm and leave somewhere warm until doubled in size.

When risen, transfer the dough to the refrigerator and leave overnight.

The next morning, tip the dough out onto a floured work surface. Knead, then weigh the dough and divide into nine equal portions. Taking each portion, fold all the edges into the centre, turn it over and roll with the palm of your hand into a ball. Roll each ball in semolina or rice flour. Take a baking tray – I use a 23 × 30 × 5cm (9 × 12 × 2 inch) one, which fits the nine rolls perfectly – and dust with a little more semolina or rice flour, then place the balls of dough on it. You want them to prove and grow into each other, so you can pull them apart when ready to eat. Cover loosely with clingfilm or a larger tin and leave until doubled in size with the edges touching one another.

Meanwhile preheat the oven to 220°C (475°F), Gas Mark 9.

Bake the rolls for 15–20 minutes until golden brown. Remove to a wire rack to cool a little, then tear apart and fill as you will.

This is the most delicious fruit loaf. It's not like a traditional bannock at all, which is said to have been invented in the 1800s by a baker in Selkirk who had excess bread dough. I bake all our bread at home and I love making this as an alternative loaf for breakfast. Using milk and butter makes for the softest dough to knead – it's quite therapeutic. I have sidestepped from tradition by using brown butter and adding walnuts. The flavours work so well together and will happily be swathed in jam or cheese – whatever takes your fancy.

Selkirk Bannock

Makes 1 loaf

- *70g (2½oz) unsalted butter, plus extra for greasing*
- *350ml (12fl oz) whole milk, plus extra for brushing*
- *10g (¼oz) caster sugar*
- *7g packet of fast-action dried yeast*
- *400g (14oz) strong white bread flour, plus extra for dusting*
- *100g (3½oz) wholemeal flour*
- *10g (¼oz) salt*
- *60g (2¼oz) beef dripping or lard*
- *50g (1¾oz) soft brown sugar*
- *Oil, for greasing*
- *300g (10½oz) sultanas*
- *75g (2¾oz) walnuts, chopped*

To serve

- *Butter, at room temperature*
- *Jam of your choice*

Melt the butter in a small pan over a medium heat, stirring with a wooden spoon for at least 5 minutes until the butter is browned and nutty in aroma. Remove from the heat and pour into a bowl to cool.

Slightly warm the milk and stir through the caster sugar and yeast. Set aside for 15 minutes to activate.

In a large bowl, mix together the flours and salt, then add the beef dripping or lard and brown sugar and rub in until the mixture resembles breadcrumbs. Add the activated yeast mixture and stir to combine. Add the cooled brown butter and mix well. Transfer the dough to a floured work surface and knead until smooth and it lightly bounces back when pressed with your finger. Add a sprinkle of flour when you need it. Place in an oiled bowl, cover and leave until doubled in size.

Push the risen dough out flat with your fingers and add most of the sultanas and all of the walnuts. Fold the dough over and knead well, then add the remaining sultanas and knead until well incorporated. Line and thoroughly butter a 22cm (8½ inch) diameter springform cake tin. Place the dough inside, cover and leave until doubled in size.

Meanwhile, preheat the oven to 200°C fan (425°F), Gas Mark 7.

Brush the surface with milk and bake for 10 minutes, then turn the heat down to 180°C fan (400°F), Gas Mark 6 and bake for a further 45 minutes.

Leave to cool in the tin for 5 minutes, then remove and place on a wire rack to cool completely. Serve with butter and a jam of your choice.

Butteries, also known as rowies, hail from the northeast of Scotland, specifically Aberdeen. They are a bit of a cross between a morning roll and a croissant, but flatter and more irregular in shape. They have a hefty addition of salt so they could stay edible for long stretches at sea for the local fishermen. These are saltier than a regular roll, but tastier for it. Savoury or sweet, these will take any flavour direction you want to take them in. Traditionally, jam is spread on the flat underside of the buttery. Crispy, sweet and salty, they are completely unique.

Butteries

Makes 12

- *7g packet of fast-action dried yeast*
- *10g (¼oz) soft brown sugar*
- *350ml (12fl oz) water at room temperature (NOT lukewarm)*
- *500g (1lb 2oz) white bread flour, plus extra for dusting*
- *20g (¾oz) salt*
- *Oil, for greasing*
- *150g (5½oz) unsalted butter, softened*
- *150g (5½oz) lard, softened*
- *Raspberry jam, to serve*

Add the yeast and brown sugar to the measured water, stir together and leave for 15 minutes to activate.

Add the flour and salt to a stand mixer fitted with a dough hook and mix lightly together before pouring in your activated yeast. Knead until the dough is very smooth and it bounces back to your touch. Transfer to an oiled bowl, cover and leave to double in size.

Meanwhile, fit the paddle attachment to the stand mixer and beat the softened butter and lard until light and fluffy like buttercream.

Tip the risen dough out onto a floured work surface and roll out to about 30 × 40cm (12 × 16 inches) and 8mm (⅜ inch) deep. With a short side facing you, spread a third of the butter and lard mixture on the bottom two-thirds of the dough, then fold in the top third of the dough and fold up the bottom third over it to cover, like folding a letter. Dust with flour. Flip so the seam is on the bottom and refrigerate for 20–30 minutes.

Repeat the rolling, spreading and folding process twice more, chilling each time. After the last refrigeration, roll out to a 32 × 24cm (12⅔ × 9½ inch) rectangle, 2cm (¾ inch) thick. Cut into 12 roughly equal squares. Taking each one, fold the corners to the centre, then flip over and dimple a bit flatter with your fingers. Place on a lined baking tray, cover with clingfilm and leave for 1 hour to rise.

Meanwhile, preheat the oven to 200°C fan (425°F), Gas Mark 7.

Bake the butteries for 15 minutes. Move to a wire rack to cool, then enjoy with raspberry jam.

The simplest of Scottish treats can be rustled up in no time. Here, I've given you a master recipe for plain scones, then listed the variations you can make from it. Really, the options are endless. Scones can be made in both a flat plate on the hob like a bannock, or in the oven, with the latter being the easier version. With all the variations, the key is to be gentle. Heavy hands make heavy scones, so try not to overwork the dough.

Scones

Makes about 6 (depending on size)

- *150ml (5fl oz) whole milk*
- *1 tablespoon vinegar (malt or white)*
- *250g (9oz) plain flour, plus extra for dusting*
- *1 teaspoon bicarbonate of soda*
- *2 teaspoons cream of tartar*
- *Pinch of salt*
- *40g (1½oz) unsalted butter, cold and cubed*
- *20g (¾oz) caster sugar*
- *1 egg, beaten*

To serve

- *Butter, at room temperature*
- *Jam of your choice*

Preheat the oven to 200°C fan (425°F), Gas Mark 7.

Mix the milk and vinegar together and leave to the side to thicken a touch while you prepare the dry ingredients. This makes a homemade buttermilk. You can use shop-bought, but I find it easiest just to make this at home with ingredients I already have.

In a large bowl, mix together the flour, bicarbonate of soda, cream of tartar and salt, then add the butter and rub it until the mixture resembles breadcrumbs. Stir through the sugar, then add your buttermilk in one go. Give it a quick stir, then tip out onto a floured work surface and gently knead until it forms a rough dough.

You can cut the dough in many ways: gently press into a rectangle or a round and cut into six pieces, or use a round cookie cutter, whatever size you like – you decide how big you want your scones to be. Space out on a baking tray, brush with beaten egg and bake for 10 minutes.

Rest on a wire rack for 5 minutes and eat warm, with jam and butter.

Baking variations

Fruit Scones
Add 100g (3½oz) sultanas just before you add the homemade buttermilk.

Treacle Scones
Replace the caster sugar with soft brown sugar and add 2 teaspoons of My Scottish 5-Spice Blend (see page 214) to the dry ingredients. Reduce the homemade buttermilk to 125ml (4fl oz) and add 25g (scant 1oz) slightly warmed black treacle along with it, whisking to combine.

Bran Scones
Use 175g (6oz) plain flour and 75g (2¾oz) wheat bran.

Cheese Scones
Omit the sugar and add 100g (3½oz) grated cheese. This could be Parmesan, a Parmesan and feta mixture, Cheddar...or anything really.

You can also add herbs, cooked spinach, bacon – just get creative. A savoury scone is magic served warm with soup.

Home Baking

9

Cream cookie is a term heard mainly in Glasgow – you may also know these as cream buns. A Scottish bakery favourite, these sweet, glazed, yeasted buns are filled with fresh cream and are perfect for afternoon tea.

Cream Cookie

Makes 16 buns

For the buns

- *550g (1lb 4oz) strong white bread flour, plus extra for dusting*
- *100g (3½oz) caster sugar*
- *10g (¼oz) salt*
- *7g packet of fast-action dried yeast*
- *125ml (4fl oz) water*
- *150ml (5fl oz) whole milk*
- *100g (3½oz) unsalted butter, melted*
- *1 egg*

For the glaze

- *2 tablespoons caster sugar*

For the filling

- *600ml (20fl oz) double cream*
- *1 teaspoon vanilla extract*
- *100g (3½oz) icing sugar*
- *Raspberry jam (optional)*

Preheat the oven to 200°C fan (425°F), Gas Mark 7. Line a couple of baking trays with nonstick baking paper.

Mix the flour, sugar and salt together in a stand mixer. Stir through the yeast, then add the measured water. In a jug, mix together the milk, butter and egg. With the mixer running on a low speed, gradually pour in the milk mixture. Increase the speed a little and mix until the dough is smooth – this will take about 10 minutes. Leave to double in size.

Move the dough to a floured work surface, split into 16 equal-sized pieces and roll into smooth balls with your hands. Place on the prepared baking trays, well-spaced, and leave to double in size.

Bake for about 15 minutes until golden.

To make the glaze, melt the sugar and 2 tablespoons water in a pan until dissolved. As soon as the buns are baked, remove them from the oven and immediately brush with the glaze. Leave to cool.

For the filling, in a large bowl, whip the cream, vanilla and icing sugar to stiff peaks. Transfer to a piping bag fitted with a star-shaped nozzle.

Cut the buns on an angle nearly all the way through. I like to spread a wee bit of raspberry jam in each bun first for a hit of tart sweetness, then generously pipe in the cream filling.

This is based on my gran's gingerbread recipe. Mum always made gingerbread when I was growing up and it was one of my favourites. There is also a famous Scottish brand of gingerbread that is decadently iced, so I have done that here with a cream cheese icing. The sweet sharpness of the icing perfectly complements the deeply sticky gingerbread to create the ultimate indulgent cake.

Iced and Spiced Fruit Gingerbread

Makes 1 × 20cm (8 inch) cake

- *250g (9oz) mixed dried fruit (I like sultanas, figs and dates)*
- *Juice of 1 orange (about 75–100ml/ 2½–3½fl oz)*
- *250g (9oz) plain flour, plus 1 tablespoon*
- *1 tablespoon ground ginger*
- *1 teaspoon My Scottish 5-Spice Blend (see page 214)*
- *1 teaspoon bicarbonate of soda*
- *Pinch of salt*
- *100g (3½oz) soft brown sugar*
- *100g (3½oz) unsalted butter*
- *200g (7oz) black treacle*
- *100ml (3½fl oz) whole milk*
- *2 eggs, beaten*

For the icing

- *250g (9oz) cream cheese*
- *50g (1¾oz) icing sugar*
- *Pinch of salt*
- *1 teaspoon ground ginger*
- *1 teaspoon vanilla extract*
- *Zest of 1 orange, plus extra to decorate*

Preheat the oven to 160°C fan (350°F), Gas Mark 4. Line a 20cm (8 inch) springform cake tin with nonstick baking paper.

Combine the dried fruit and orange juice in a pan and gently heat until warm (or do this in a microwave). Set aside for at least 1 hour.

Sift the 250g (9oz) flour, spices and bicarbonate of soda into a large bowl, add the salt and sugar and mix to combine.

In a small pan, melt the butter and treacle until well combined, then mix in the milk. Leave to cool slightly, then add to the flour mixture along with the eggs and stir well to combine. Pour any residual liquid from the fruit into the batter, then toss the fruit pieces in the extra tablespoon of flour. Fold the fruit into the batter, then pour into the prepared cake tin.

Bake for 50–55 minutes, or until a skewer inserted into the cake comes out clean. Leave to cool in the tin for about 30 minutes, then remove to a wire rack to cool completely.

When cool, make the icing. In a large bowl, whip together all the ingredients until smooth. Pipe or spread generously on top of the cake and decorate with extra orange zest.

This cake is just as delicious without icing and also gets better after being stored in an airtight container for a couple of days, becoming super moist, sticky and full of flavour. Serve it warm with ice cream or just alongside a good cup of tea – perfect comfort in each bite.

Parlies is short for parliament cakes. These biscuits originated in the 18th century, served in a café opposite the Scottish Parliament Building in Edinburgh. They are like an early ginger snap. Treacle and ginger give them their flavour and colour, and they are rolled into a sheet and cut into squares. Traditionally consumed with a wee dram of whisky, these days they are more often accompanied by a cup of tea. I have added an extra touch of some ginger icing with 'Glasgow Jam', an old Scottish name for hundreds and thousands sprinkles.

Parlies

Make 24 biscuits (plus ragged edges!)

- *200g (7oz) plain flour*
- *100g (3½oz) soft brown sugar*
- *20g (¾oz) ground ginger*
- *1 teaspoon bicarbonate of soda*
- *Pinch of salt*
- *100g (3½oz) unsalted butter*
- *50g (1¾oz) black treacle*

For the ginger icing

- *50g (1¾oz) icing sugar*
- *½ teaspoon My Scottish 5-Spice Blend (see page 214), or use ground ginger*
- *2 teaspoons milk or water, or as needed*
- *Hundreds and thousands sprinkles, to decorate*

Preheat the oven to 180°C fan (400°F), Gas Mark 6.

In a large bowl, mix together the flour, sugar, ginger, bicarbonate of soda and salt.

In a small pan, melt together the butter and treacle, then add to the flour mixture. Mix thoroughly, then bring together with your hands.

Transfer the ball of dough to the work surface and sandwich between 2 sheets of greaseproof paper. Roll out to 5mm (¼ inch) thick, leaving the edges ragged. Remove the top piece of paper and use the bottom sheet to transfer the dough to a baking tray. Using a sharp knife or pizza cutter, divide the dough into 24 square biscuits.

Bake for 10 minutes.

While still warm, run the knife over the lines again, then use a palette knife to carefully move each biscuit to a wire rack to cool and crisp up.

To make the icing, stir together the icing sugar, 5-Spice Blend and milk or water to a thick dropping consistency. Dip the face of each biscuit into the icing. While the icing is still wet, sprinkle with hundreds and thousands, then leave to dry.

Serve this decorated version alongside a cup of tea – or leave them plain and pair with a dram of whisky. Try it out and enjoy a wee piece of Scottish history.

Seed cake has a long history in Scotland, but it was popular all across Britain from the early 18th century. This is a recipe that has been handed down to me from a family friend – it originally belonged to her Scottish grandmother. Caraway seeds are used in a number of peculiarly Scottish dishes, most notably petticoat tail shortbread, which is said to have been enjoyed by Mary, Queen of Scots. Although you can buy ground caraway, I like to toast caraway seeds myself until fragrant before grinding to a powder and adding to the cake. I have included the flavours of orange in this cake, turning it into a kind of caraway orange drizzle cake. Soft, moist and deeply fragranced, it could easily work as a dessert with a good dollop of cream, but it's also delicious for breakfast with a coffee.

Seed Cake

Makes 1 × 20cm (8 inch) cake

- *150g (5½oz) unsalted butter*
- *150g (5½oz) caster sugar*
- *3 eggs*
- *150g (5½oz) plain flour*
- *2 teaspoons baking powder*
- *Zest of 1 orange*
- *Pinch of salt*
- *2 tablespoons lightly toasted caraway seeds, ground to a powder*
- *3 tablespoons whole milk*
- *Whipped cream, to serve*

For the drizzle topping

- *100g (3½oz) caster sugar*
- *Juice of 1 orange*
- *1 teaspoon lightly toasted caraway seeds, ground to a powder*

Preheat the oven to 180°C fan (400°F), Gas Mark 6. Line a 20cm (8 inch) springform cake tin with nonstick baking paper.

Cream the butter and sugar until light and fluffy. Add the eggs, one at a time, with a spoonful of flour, mixing well between each addition. When it's all incorporated, add the rest of the flour along with the baking powder, orange zest, salt, ground caraway seeds and milk. Fold through until well combined.

Pour the batter into the prepared tin and bake for 30 minutes.

Meanwhile, make your drizzle topping. Add all the ingredients to a bowl and let the sugar dissolve.

When the cake is done, remove from the oven and poke holes all over the top with a skewer. Pour over the drizzle and leave to cool in the tin before removing, slicing and serving with a dollop of cream. Alternatively, it is delightful served still slightly warm, with custard.

A popular bakery slice, this is where a Bakewell tart meets an almond slice, with some dried fruit and a frangipane sponge top. I have used my simple oat and almond pastry for the base, which does not need to be par-baked, making it very quick and simple to assemble.

Paradise Slice

Makes 8–10 slices

For the pastry base

- *100g (3½oz) unsalted butter, melted, plus extra for greasing*
- *100g (3½oz) almond flour*
- *100g (3½oz) oat flour (or use rolled oats blitzed to a flour)*
- *50g (1¾oz) icing sugar*
- *½ teaspoon salt*

For the frangipane filling

- *100g (3½oz) glacé cherries, finely chopped*
- *100g (3½oz) currants or sultanas (or a mix of both)*
- *1 tablespoon almond flour*
- *150g (5½oz) butter, softened*
- *150g (5½oz) caster sugar, plus extra for sprinkling*
- *2 eggs*
- *50g (1¾oz) plain flour*
- *100g (3½oz) ground almonds*
- *½ teaspoon salt*
- *Drop of almond extract*
- *100g (3½oz) raspberry jam (or any flavour you prefer), or as needed*

Grease a 35 × 14½cm (14 × 5¾ inch) tart tin with butter and line with nonstick baking paper. Mix all the ingredients for the pastry base together in a bowl, then press by hand into the prepared tin. Make sure to press into the corners and leave no gaps. It will all fit, just take your time, then use a palette knife to flatten as neatly as possible. Pop into the freezer for 30 minutes.

Preheat the oven to 160°C fan (350°F), Gas Mark 4.

To make the filling, place the cherries and currants or sultanas in a bowl and toss them all in the almond flour.

In a separate bowl, beat the butter and sugar until light and fluffy, then add the eggs, one at a time, with a spoonful of plain flour, mixing until well incorporated. Stir through the remaining plain flour, with the ground almonds and salt. Add the floured fruit and almond extract and fold through.

Take the pastry base out of the freezer. Cover the entire base with the jam, then top with the fruity frangipane filling. Use a palette knife to smooth it to all the edges.

Bake for 50–55 minutes, or until an inserted skewer comes out clean. Immediately on removing from the oven, sprinkle the surface with caster sugar, then leave to cool in the tin.

When cool, remove carefully from the tin, cut into fingers and serve.

This popular traybake, seen regularly at coffee mornings and in garden centre cafés, was one of my absolute favourites growing up. The shortbread gets its name from its additional 'rich' layers of caramel and chocolate. Adding toppings to shortbread dates back to at least the 19th century but this version was popularized in the 1970s, which is why it is so prominent in my memories.

Millionaire Shortbread

Makes 24 squares

For the shortbread

- *150g (5½oz) unsalted butter, softened, plus extra for greasing*
- *150g (5½oz) plain flour, sifted, plus extra for dusting*
- *50g (1¾oz) cornflour, sifted*
- *100g (3½oz) caster sugar*
- *Pinch of salt*

For the caramel

- *150g (5½oz) unsalted butter*
- *150g (5½oz) soft brown sugar*
- *395g (14oz) can sweetened condensed milk*
- *3 tablespoons golden syrup*
- *1 teaspoon smoked salt flakes*
- *Few drops of vanilla extract*

For the chocolate topping

- *85g (3oz) dark chocolate*
- *85g (3oz) milk chocolate*
- *1 teaspoon neutral oil*
- *Smoked salt flakes, for sprinkling*

Preheat the oven to 160°C fan (350°F), Gas Mark 4. Grease a 26 × 20cm (10½ × 8 inch) baking tin.

Combine all the shortbread ingredients in a stand mixer fitted with a paddle attachment and mix until just combined. Roll the dough out on a floured work surface to a rectangle the size of your tin. Place it in the tin, ensuring it fills each corner. Prick all over with a fork and bake for 20 minutes. Leave to cool in the tin.

For the caramel, melt the butter in a saucepan over a low heat, then add the sugar, condensed milk and golden syrup. Stirring constantly, let the mixture cook for at least 20 minutes until darker in colour and visibly thickened. You should see it start to pull away from the edges of the pan. Add the salt and vanilla and mix well. Carefully pour the caramel over the shortbread base and tap the tin on the worktop to distribute it evenly. Pop into the refrigerator to allow the caramel to set.

To make the topping, melt both chocolates in a heatproof bowl set over a pan of boiling water. Stir through the oil. Pour the chocolate topping over the surface of the caramel, spreading it to the edges, then give it a few gentle taps on the worktop to even it out. Sprinkle with a little smoked salt and place in the refrigerator to set.

Once set, carefully run a sharp knife round the edge to loosen the shortbread from the tin and carefully turn out onto a board. Cut into squares and sprinkle with a little extra salt, if desired.

A yum yum was always one of my absolute bakery favourites. Completely decadent, it's a twisted doughnut covered with a thin icing. This version, based on the original, borrows from another Scottish bakery classic – the toffee doughnut. These yum yums are covered with a toffee icing, combining the best of these two iconic treats (see photograph overleaf). I seem to sprinkle salt on everything sweet, but these really do benefit from a touch of smoked salt.

Toffee Yum Yums

Makes 8

- *7g packet of fast-action dried yeast*
- *35g (1¼oz) caster sugar*
- *75ml (2½fl oz) water at room temperature*
- *350g (12oz) strong bread flour, plus extra for dusting*
- *7g (⅜oz) salt*
- *150ml (5fl oz) whole milk, at room temperature*
- *1 egg, whisked*
- *75g (2¾oz) frozen unsalted butter, grated*
- *Vegetable or rapeseed oil, for deep-frying*
- *Smoked salt, to decorate*

In a small bowl, add the yeast and 1 teaspoon of the sugar to the measured water, stir and leave to bloom.

Add the flour, salt and the remaining sugar to a stand mixer fitted with a dough hook (or use a mixing bowl and spoon) and mix briefly. Keep the motor running and add the milk and the whisked egg, followed by the bloomed yeast and water. Mix until well combined, then add the grated butter and mix briefly.

Turn the mixture out onto a floured work surface, sprinkle a little more flour over the top and gently knead until the stickiness has gone. Pop the dough into a clean bowl, cover with a tea towel and set aside to rest for 30 minutes.

Remove the dough from the bowl and roll out on a floured work surface to about 20 × 30cm (8 × 12 inches). With a short side facing you, fold the top edge down by a third and the bottom edge up by a third to cover it. Rotate 90 degrees, then roll out in the same way and repeat the fold. Place on a silicone mat or a baking tray lined with greaseproof paper, cover with clingfilm and place in the refrigerator for 30 minutes.

Remove the dough from the refrigerator and repeat the above process again. Cover and return to the refrigerator for 1 hour.

On a floured work surface, roll the chilled dough out to a 32 × 20cm (12⅔ × 8 inch) rectangle, then cut into eight strips. Make a slit in the middle of each strip, almost to the ends but leaving each end attached. Twist the middle sections around each other to create the signature yum yum shape. Return to the mat or lined tray, cover and leave in a warm place until doubled in size.

For the toffee icing

- *35g (1¼oz) unsalted butter*
- *35g (1¼oz) soft brown sugar*
- *4 tablespoons whole milk, or as needed*
- *150g (5½oz) icing sugar, or as needed*

Meanwhile, make the toffee icing. In a small pan, melt the butter with the sugar and let it caramelize for a few minutes. Stir in the milk, then add the icing sugar and stir well to combine. You can add more milk if you want it thinner, or more icing sugar for a thicker icing. Set aside.

Heat enough oil for deep-frying in a deep, heavy-based pan or a deep-fat fryer to 180°C (350°F), or until a cube of dough browns in 30 seconds. I recommend using a thermometer to ensure the oil stays at a constant temperature. Working in small batches, carefully lower each yum yum into the hot oil and fry for about 2 minutes on each side until golden. Remove with a slotted spoon to a wire rack set over a tray.

While the yum yums are still warm, generously brush the toffee icing all over them on both sides. Sprinkle with a little smoked salt for delicious salted caramel overtones.

The pineapple tart is a Scottish bakery classic. As iconic as the strawberry tart, it will frequently make an appearance in the goodie box we treat ourselves to when back in Glasgow. I think this is one of the most fun and delicious things that you can do with a can of pineapple – it's used in every part of the recipe from the pastry to the icing (see photograph on previous page).

Pineapple Tarts

Makes 10–12 tarts

- *440g (15½oz) can pineapple slices*

For the pastry

- *200g (7oz) plain flour*
- *1 tablespoon caster sugar*
- *Pinch of salt*
- *100g (3½oz) unsalted butter, cubed, plus extra for greasing*
- *1 teaspoon vanilla extract*
- *2 egg yolks, plus 1 whole egg*

Drain the juice from the can of pineapple and reserve. Finely chop the pineapple. Strain the residual juice from the pineapple and keep to one side.

For the pastry, place the flour, sugar and salt into a stand mixer and mix briefly. Add the butter and mix until it has the consistency of breadcrumbs. Add the vanilla, the 2 egg yolks and 2 tablespoons of the reserved pineapple juice. Mix to bring it together. Tip out onto the work surface and knead gently to form a flat circle. Wrap in clingfilm and rest in the refrigerator for at least 15 minutes.

Meanwhile, preheat the oven to 160°C fan (350°F), Gas Mark 4. Grease the bottom of an upturned cupcake or muffin tin with butter.

Unwrap the dough and roll out to 4mm (¼ inch) thick. Use a 9cm (3½ inch) round cutter to cut out 10–12 discs and place them over the cups of the upturned cupcake or muffin tin. Place another cupcake tin over the top to weight the pastry down and bake for 15 minutes. Remove from the oven and turn the tart shells the right way up, placing them into the cups of the cupcake or muffin tin.

In a food processor, blend the leftover pastry (this will be about 50g/1¾oz) with the whole egg and 1 tablespoon of the reserved pineapple juice, then brush this mixture over the inside of the tart shells before placing them back in the oven for about 7 minutes until lightly golden.

For the Swiss meringue buttercream

- *2 egg whites*
- *Caster sugar (same weight as egg whites, see method)*
- *⅛ teaspoon cream of tartar*
- *1 teaspoon vanilla extract*
- *Pinch of salt*
- *125g (4½oz) unsalted butter, cubed, at room temperature*

For the icing

- *250g (9oz) icing sugar*
- *Few drops of yellow food colouring*

For the Swiss meringue buttercream, weigh the egg whites and measure out the same weight of caster sugar. Place in a heatproof bowl with the cream of tartar. Whisk together, then place the bowl over a pan of simmering water and continue whisking until quite warm to the touch. When a little mixture is rubbed between your fingers there should be no residual graininess. Transfer to a stand mixer and start whisking slowly. Increase the speed until glossy peaks are formed. Add the vanilla and salt and whisk again to combine. Remove a spoonful and reserve for the icing, then add the butter to the bowl, cube by cube, whisking all the time until fully incorporated and silky smooth. Alternatively, you could use a hand whisk. Transfer to a piping bag fitted with a nozzle.

For the icing, sift the icing sugar into a bowl, add 2 tablespoons of the reserved pineapple juice, the food colouring and the reserved meringue. Mix together, adding a little more food colouring and more pineapple juice until you reach your desired shade and have a thick pouring consistency.

To assemble the tarts, place 1 heaped teaspoon of chopped pineapple in each pastry shell. Pipe buttercream on top to cover, then drizzle over the icing, covering the buttercream and letting it pool around the inside of the pastry shell. Let the tarts set, then enjoy.

In Scotland, local garden centres often have a lovely café, full of home-baked treats. The peppermint slice was my go-to when visiting ours. The amount of green colouring and peppermint flavour is up to you, but I have given a guide below. It's well balanced with the bitterness of the dark chocolate, but I also like to decorate mine with mint chocolate bars bashed to smithereens!

Peppermint Slice

Makes 24 squares

For the base

- *150g (5½oz) unsalted butter, melted, plus extra for greasing*
- *125g (4½oz) self-raising flour*
- *100g (3½oz) soft brown sugar*
- *50g (1¾oz) cornflakes, crushed*
- *2 tablespoons cocoa powder*
- *¼ teaspoon salt*
- *1 teaspoon vanilla extract*

For the fondant

- *500g (1lb 2oz) icing sugar*
- *½ tablespoon peppermint extract*
- *Tiny drop of green food colouring (optional)*

For the topping

- *150g (5½oz) dark chocolate*
- *1 teaspoon neutral oil*
- *125g (4½oz) mint chocolate*

Preheat the oven to 180°C fan (400°F), Gas Mark 6. Grease a 26 × 20cm (10½ × 8 inch) baking tin with butter and line with greaseproof paper.

For the base, combine the flour, sugar, crushed cornflakes, cocoa and salt in a bowl. Add the melted butter and vanilla and mix to a dough. Press into the prepared tin and bake for 15 minutes. Allow to cool completely.

To make the fondant, sift the icing sugar into a bowl, then add the peppermint and 3 tablespoons cold water and stir well to combine. To add the food colouring, dip a cocktail stick into the colour, then wipe into the icing. Mix it up and keep doing that until you reach your desired depth of colour. Spread the fondant over the cooled biscuit base, then refrigerate until firmed up.

To make the topping, melt the dark chocolate in a heatproof bowl set over a pan of boiling water, then stir through the oil. Spread the topping over the fondant layer. Bash up the mint chocolate with a rolling pin, then sprinkle over the chocolate layer. Refrigerate overnight for best results.

When set, cut into squares with a sharp knife.

Created in Scotland in the early 20th century, Scottish chocolate tiffin is traditionally a no-bake slice that sets in the refrigerator. This popular Malteser version is the next level up. I have leaned into the malty flavours by using malted milk biscuits and malted milk drinking powder. This is officially now my favourite chocolate bar.

Malteser Tiffin

Makes 24 squares

For the base

- *100g (3½oz) dark chocolate*
- *100g (3½oz) milk chocolate*
- *40g (1½oz) unsalted butter*
- *395g (14oz) can sweetened condensed milk*
- *250g (9oz) malted milk biscuits*
- *200g (7oz) Maltesers, plus extra to decorate*
- *90g (3¼oz) dates, chopped*
- *3 tablespoons malted milk powder (I use Horlicks), plus extra to decorate*

For the chocolate topping

- *100g (3½oz) milk chocolate*
- *100g (3½oz) dark chocolate*
- *20g (¾oz) unsalted butter*

Grease a 28 × 20cm (11 × 8 inch) baking tin and line it with greaseproof paper.

Melt the chocolates and butter together in a large pan over a low heat, then add the condensed milk and stir well. Remove from the heat.

Place the biscuits in a bag and start to break them up with a rolling pin, then add half of the Maltesers and continue to bash. Add the crushed mixture to the melted chocolate mixture along with the remaining whole Maltesers and the chopped dates. Mix well, then add the malted milk powder and mix thoroughly. Tip into the prepared tin and press to the edges, using a spatula to level out the surface. Place in the refrigerator to set.

To make the topping, melt the chocolates and butter in a heatproof bowl set over a pan of boiling water until well combined. Pour over the base and tap the tin on the worktop to even the surface out. Dot extra Maltesers over the surface, then place back in the refrigerator to set.

When ready to serve, cut into squares, then sprinkle with a little extra malted milk powder. These are honestly so good – the chewiness of the dates with the crunch of the whole Maltesers is just the best.

Tablet is a sugary Scottish treat. If you want to wind up a Scottish person, call it fudge! Fudge it certainly is not. Tablet has a medium-hard bite and melts in the mouth. It's delicious. My mum used to make it all the time. It's very easy, but timing is key – pour it out before it's ready and it will be a sticky toffee mess. If you don't stir it frequently, it can stick to the pan and burn. And be watchful – it can very easily boil over if the heat is too high.

Tablet

Makes about 70 small squares

- *900g (2lb) golden caster sugar (regular is fine, too)*
- *115g (4oz) unsalted butter*
- *395g (14oz) can sweetened condensed milk*
- *400ml (14fl oz) whole milk (fill the empty condensed milk can)*

Add all the ingredients to a really large saucepan and heat very gently, stirring constantly with a wooden spoon, until the butter is melted and everything is amalgamated. Keep an eye on it – you don't want the sugar to start to caramelize. When it reaches boiling point, turn it down to a steady simmer and cook for at least 1 hour, stirring occasionally. It will go through several colour changes before it's ready and it always takes longer than you think, so be patient and take care, as the mixture will be boiling hot. As it begins to darken, stir continuously until it smells distinctively of caramel and the spoon starts to leave a visible trail. When it reaches a dark caramel colour and has thickened up nicely, it is ready.

Remove from the heat and beat with an electric whisk for 4–5 minutes, then quickly tip the mixture into a nonstick, 28 × 18cm (11 × 7 inch) baking tin. Tap the tin on the worktop to level the mixture out. While it is still hot, use a knife to score the surface of the tablet gently into small squares. Leave to cool.

When cool, break into squares and enjoy. It is particularly special with a coffee or a cup of tea.

I cannot remember life without digestives – they have been around forever! Invented in the early 18th century in Scotland by two doctors, primarily to aid digestion, they were first produced commercially in the late 19th century. An incredibly popular biscuit, ubiquitous in a household biscuit tin, they are perfect for dunking in your cup of tea and also work brilliantly on a cheeseboard.

Digestive Biscuits

Makes 18 biscuits

- *140g (5oz) unsalted butter*
- *85g (3oz) soft brown sugar*
- *1 egg*
- *1 tablespoon malt extract*
- *½ teaspoon salt*
- *½ teaspoon bicarbonate of soda*
- *½ teaspoon tartaric acid (or vinegar)*
- *250g (9oz) plain wholemeal flour, plus extra for dusting*

In a large bowl, cream the butter and sugar until light and fluffy. Add the egg and malt extract and beat together until roughly combined. Add the salt, bicarbonate of soda, tartaric acid and flour and beat until well combined.

Turn out onto a floured work surface and bring together into a flat disc, then wrap in clingfilm and refrigerate for 30 minutes.

Preheat the oven to 160°C fan (350°F), Gas Mark 4. Line several baking trays with nonstick baking paper.

Cut the dough in half and roll out to about 5mm (¼ inch) thick. Use a 7cm (2¾ inch) round cookie cutter to cut into biscuits and stamp the surfaces, if you have a cookie stamper. Repeat until all the dough has been used up. Place the biscuits onto the lined trays.

Bake for 12–15 minutes until golden and crisp, then remove to a wire rack to cool.

Store in an airtight container.

These biscuits are one of the most popular in the UK. I survived on them when I was at college, along with many, many cups of tea. The love child of a digestive and a flapjack, these oaty biscuits are easy to make at home and come together in no time. Great on their own, or – my personal favourite – coated on top with melted milk or dark chocolate.

Chocolate 'Hob Nobs'

Makes 15 biscuits

- *150g (5½oz) instant (quick-cook) oats (see Note, below)*
- *50g (1¾oz) plain flour*
- *50g (1¾oz) wholemeal flour*
- *85g (3oz) caster sugar*
- *½ teaspoon salt*
- *1 teaspoon bicarbonate of soda*
- *150g (5½oz) unsalted butter*
- *2 heaped tablespoons golden syrup*
- *100g (3½oz) milk or dark chocolate, melted (optional)*

Preheat the oven to 180°C fan (400°F), Gas Mark 6. Line a couple of baking trays with nonstick baking paper.

Combine the dry ingredients in a large bowl.

In a small pan, melt the butter and golden syrup together, then pour over the dry ingredients. Mix until well combined. Place tablespoons of the mixture on the prepared tray, then use a glass to lightly flatten the tops. Using the open end of the glass, birl it around the mixture to make neat little circles.

Bake for 10 minutes for a crispy edge and slightly chewy middle. If you like them crisp all the way through, bake at 160°C fan (350°F), Gas Mark 4, for 20 minutes instead, keeping a close eye on them.

When they are still hot, lightly flatten, then birl the biscuits again into neat round shapes using a glass or a cookie cutter. Transfer to a wire rack to cool.

If you like, coat the tops with the melted chocolate of your choice.

Note: Instant or quick-cook oats are essential to this recipe. Rolled or porridge oats just won't work. If that's all you have, give them a quick pulse in a food processor to break them down into much smaller flakes, then continue with the method above.

Scotland has the nickname 'Land of Cakes' and it doesn't disappoint with choice. This sultana cake is one of many tea cakes that litter Scottish baking history and grace many a morning tea table. So simple to put together, I have livened mine up with citrus notes – lemon zest, mixed peel and orange-infused olive oil. You could use regular olive oil and a splash of orange or lemon essence, if you like. The citrus notes contribute not only to a delightful baking aroma but really elevate this simple cake to one you won't be able to stop eating – it is one of my favourites.

Sultana Cake

Makes 1 × 20cm (8 inch) square cake

- *1 lemon*
- *1 orange*
- *250g (9oz) sultanas*
- *150g (5½oz) unsalted butter*
- *150g (5½oz) caster sugar*
- *3 eggs*
- *250g (9oz) plain flour*
- *2 teaspoons baking powder*
- *Pinch of salt*
- *50g (1¾oz) mixed peel*
- *1 tablespoon orange-infused olive oil*
- *Demerara sugar, for sprinkling*

Preheat the oven to 180°C fan (400°F), Gas Mark 6. Grease and line a 20cm (8 inch) square cake tin with nonstick baking paper.

Zest the lemon and orange and set the zest to one side, then juice the fruit into a bowl. Add the sultanas to the juice. Heat through in the microwave (or in a small pan) until warm, then cover and leave for 15 minutes–1 hour while you prepare the sponge.

In a large bowl, cream the butter and sugar until pale and fluffy. Add the eggs, one at a time, along with a spoonful of flour, beating well after each addition. Add the baking powder, the remaining flour and the salt. Mix very slowly until just combined – do not overbeat at this stage. Add the mixed peel, drain the sultanas and add them, then add the citrus zests followed by the olive oil. Fold through until the fruit is well distributed, then pour the batter into the prepared tin, spreading it out gently with a spatula into the corners. Sprinkle the top with Demerara sugar.

Bake for 30 minutes, or until an inserted skewer comes out clean. Leave to cool in the tin, then slice and enjoy.

This is an heirloom recipe and one that I am sure everyone makes differently. The version below is my mum's, and she is to shortbread as Italian nonnas are to pasta. She can make this in her sleep and it's perfect every time. This 'biscuit' style is not traditional, but it is addictively crumbly and delicious, and is now my preferred way to eat shortbread. If you want to take these a step further, try making the whisky caramel for chocolate-edged shortbread sandwiches – they are devilishly good.

Mum's Shortbread

Makes about 40 biscuits

- *250g (9oz) unsalted butter, softened*
- *250g (9oz) plain flour, plus extra for dusting*
- *125g (4½oz) cornflour*
- *100g (3½oz) caster sugar, plus extra for sprinkling*
- *25g (scant 1oz) icing sugar*

For the whisky caramel (optional)

- *200g (7oz) caster sugar*
- *100ml (3½fl oz) double cream*
- *2 teaspoons whisky*
- *2 teaspoons butter*
- *½ teaspoon smoked salt flakes*
- *100g (3½oz) dark chocolate*
- *¼ teaspoon smoked salt flakes*

Preheat the oven to 160°C fan (350°F), Gas Mark 4. Line a couple of baking trays with nonstick baking paper.

Put all the shortbread ingredients in a stand mixer and mix until they clump together. When this happens, stop the mixer immediately – do not continue to mix. Push the dough together with your hands and divide in half. Sprinkle the work surface with a little flour and roll the dough out to about 5mm (¼ inch) thick. Use a circular cookie cutter to cut into biscuits and place on the prepared baking trays. Prick all over the surface with a fork. You can gather and re-roll the scraps to make more biscuits.

Bake for 15 minutes. They shouldn't brown, just turn an even pale colour all over. Remove to a wire rack to cool, then dust with a sprinkling of caster sugar. They are delicious just as they are, but to take them to the next level, follow the optional step below.

To make the whisky caramel, heat the sugar gently in a pan until it has dissolved and turned a rich caramel colour. Add the cream and whisky and stir until all lumps have dissolved, then stir through the butter. Pour into a bowl to cool and stir through the smoked salt flakes. When cool, transfer to a piping bag and pipe onto the bottom side of half of the shortbread biscuits, then sandwich with another biscuit. For the chocolate finish, melt the chocolate in the microwave, stir through the smoked salt flakes and carefully roll the biscuit sandwich edges in it until they are all sealed. Pop on a plate and into the refrigerator for 5–10 minutes to set.

This is another Scottish bakery classic. Two shortbread biscuits are sandwiched together with raspberry jam, then dipped into a simple icing and topped with a glacé cherry (or a jelly sweet, depending on your bakery). Originally called German biscuits, they were renamed Empire biscuits during World War I, but you might also see them named double biscuits. I use whole egg in the shortbread dough, but my gran's recipe, on which this is based, uses dried egg – that's how old it is.

Empire Biscuits

Makes 12 biscuits

For the dough

- *115g (4oz) salted butter*
- *115g (4oz) icing sugar*
- *1 egg*
- *½ teaspoon vanilla extract*
- *225g (8oz) plain flour*

For the icing

- *175g (6oz) icing sugar*
- *2 teaspoons water, or as needed*

To decorate

- *Raspberry jam or my Jam with a Dram (see page 219)*
- *6 glacé cherries, halved, or 12 jelly sweets*

In a large bowl, cream the butter and sugar until light and fluffy, then add the egg and mix well. Add the vanilla and flour and bring the dough together. Don't overbeat, just let it come together, then tip out of the bowl and push together by hand. Form into a flattish circle, wrap in clingfilm and chill in the refrigerator for 30 minutes.

Meanwhile, preheat the oven to 180°C fan (400°F), Gas Mark 6. Line a couple of baking trays with nonstick baking paper.

Remove from the refrigerator and roll out to 5mm (¼ inch) thick. I find it easier to cut the dough in half before rolling out, as it makes it easier to manage. Cut out biscuits with a fluted cookie cutter and place on the prepared baking trays. You can reform and roll the scraps to make more biscuits.

Bake for 10 minutes until slightly golden around the edges. Transfer to a wire rack to cool.

To make the icing, sift the icing sugar into a bowl and add the water a little at a time, mixing until it comes together in a thick icing.

When cool, spread jam on the bottom side of half of the biscuits, then sandwich with the other biscuits. Carefully dip one face of each biscuit sandwich into the icing, then twist as you turn it over and leave to settle. Pop half a glacé cherry or a whole jelly sweet on top of each one before the icing sets.

Swally
Cocktails and Drinks

10

Spiced Irn-Bru and Orange Syrup

Add a little unexpected Celtic complexity to your cocktails with this brilliant cocktail syrup! It may seem like a bit of a joke, but the fruity quality of Irn-Bru actually goes perfectly with orange and spices, making it a legitimately good cocktail addition. Not just for Burns Night, this syrup will add a real Scottish twist to some of your favourite cocktails.

Makes 500ml (18fl oz)

- *4 × 330ml (11fl oz) cans of Irn-Bru*
- *150g (5½oz) granulated sugar*
- *Pared zest of 1 orange*
- *Juice of 3 oranges*
- *1 cinnamon stick*
- *Thumb-sized piece of fresh root ginger, peeled and sliced*
- *5 cloves*
- *1 teaspoon allspice berries*
- *1 teaspoon juniper berries*

Combine all the ingredients in a pan, bring to the boil and reduce to between half and one-third of the original amount. Strain, then decant into a clean bottle and leave to cool. I store mine in the refrigerator and it lasts for months.

Spiced Irn-Bru Whisky Sour

Serves 1

- *30ml (2 tablespoons) blended Scotch whisky*
- *30ml (2 tablespoons) Spiced Irn-Bru and Orange Syrup (see above)*
- *2 tablespoons lemon juice*
- *1 tablespoon egg white*
- *Ice*
- *1 maraschino cherry, to decorate*

Put all the ingredients into a cocktail shaker filled with ice and shake vigorously. Strain out the ice and shake again. Strain into a tumbler filled with ice and decorate with a maraschino cherry.

Spiced Irn-Bru Sbagliato

Serves 1

- *Ice*
- *30ml (2 tablespoons) Campari*
- *30ml (2 tablespoons) Spiced Irn-Bru and Orange Syrup (see page 204)*
- *60ml (4 tablespoons) Prosecco*
- *Slice of fresh orange, to garnish*

Half-fill a tumbler or a stemmed wine glass with ice, then pour over the liquid ingredients. Give everything a quick swizzle around to mix and serve with a slice of orange and a straw.

Spiced Irn-Bru Spritz

Serves 1

- *Ice*
- *20ml (4 teaspoons) Spiced Irn-Bru and Orange Syrup (see page 204)*
- *20ml (4 teaspoons) Aperol*
- *80ml (5½ tablespoons) Prosecco*
- *Splash of soda water*
- *Slice of fresh or dried blood orange, to decorate*

Fill a stemmed wine glass with ice, add all the liquid ingredients and stir. Decorate with a slice of blood orange.

Spiced Irn-Bru Negroni

Serves 1

- *Ice*
- *30ml (2 tablespoons) Campari*
- *30ml (2 tablespoons) Scottish gin*
- *15ml (1 tablespoon) Spiced Irn-Bru and Orange Syrup (see page 204)*
- *Slice of fresh orange, to decorate*

Fill a tumbler with ice and pour over the liquid ingredients. Stir well with a long spoon and decorate with a slice of fresh orange.

Auld-Fashioned

Serves 1

- *Ice*
- *20ml (4 teaspoons) Spiced Irn-Bru and Orange Syrup (see page 204)*
- *Good dash of orange bitters*
- *60ml (4 tablespoons) blended Scotch whisky*
- *Strip of pared orange zest*
- *1 maraschino cherry, to decorate*

Half-fill a glass with ice. Add all the liquid ingredients and stir well. Spritz the orange zest over the cocktail and rub it around the rim of the glass. Decorate with a maraschino cherry.

Polished Nail

This is a refined version of a Rusty Nail, one of the simplest of Scottish cocktails and one of my all-time favourites. Avid whisky drinkers may shudder at this, but I love the flavour a single malt brings over a blend – and it gives you much more choice over the flavour profile.

Serves 1

- *30ml (2 tablespoons) single malt whisky*
- *30ml (2 tablespoons) Drambuie*
- *Ice*
- *Dash or two of orange bitters*
- *Pared strip of orange zest, to decorate*

Pour the spirits over ice, splash on a few drops of orange bitters and stir with a long spoon. Decorate with a freshly pared strip of orange zest.

Lime Cordial

The best-known and OG lime cordial – Rose's – was invented by Lachlan Rose, a ship chandler from Leith in Edinburgh. Due to the high vitamin C content, lime juice preserved with rum was given to sailors in the British Navy to prevent and cure scurvy. Rose realized in 1865 that preserving limes with sugar opened up a larger market and patented his method in 1867. It was the world's first commercially produced fruit concentrate.

I grew up drinking this and most people I know would attest to Rose's being the only brand they buy. I thought it would be fun to make some and I used a lot more lime juice than the original! Of course, you can tailor the sweetness to suit your taste. I like it quite sharp and not too sweet. It's very refreshing, especially on a hot day, served over ice with sparkling water and decorated with ginger and fresh mint.

Makes 700ml (1¼ pints)

- *10 limes, washed and dried*
- *225g (8oz) caster sugar (or to taste)*
- *225ml (8fl oz) water*
- *2 teaspoons citric acid*

Finely grate the lime zest into a bowl. Next juice the limes, then weigh the resulting juice. Mine came to 460g (just over 1lb). Weigh out 50–100 per cent of that weight in sugar, depending on the sweetness of your tooth (I think 50 per cent is enough). Pour the juice over the lime zest and mix in the sugar until dissolved.

Dissolve the citric acid into 230g (just over 8oz) water (half of the juice weight), then pour into the lime mixture. Cover and leave overnight to infuse.

The next day, strain the mixture through a fine-mesh sieve into a clean bottle and store in the refrigerator for up to 1 month.

Bramble Highlander

This is a refreshing wee cocktail inspired by bramble picking with my mum. Mint and thyme bring herbal notes, and the elderflower liqueur ties it together with a touch of sweetness.

Serves 1

- *4 blackberries (brambles)*
- *2 sprigs of thyme*
- *1 tablespoon elderflower liqueur*
- *60ml (4 tablespoons) Scottish gin*
- *Ice*
- *Soda water, to top up*
- *Sprig of mint, to garnish*

In a cocktail shaker, muddle 3 blackberries and 1 thyme sprig with the elderflower liqueur. Add the gin and a scoop of ice and shake. Let it loosen for a minute, then shake again.

Strain into a tumbler over ice and top up with soda water. Garnish with the other sprig of thyme, the mint and remaining blackberry.

Batch Scottish Martini

Making a batch martini is great, especially if you have guests coming. I do love the crafting of a martini on the spot, but by making this and freezing it ahead of time, the viscosity is changed to something more syrupy, smooth and unctuous. You can experiment with different gins and vermouths to create a variety of flavour profiles. I often like the mix of two different vermouths or sometimes even a wee splash of bergamot liqueur. Simply pour into chilled glasses and spritz with lemon zest – very classy.

Makes 1 × 70cl (23fl oz) bottle

- *450ml (16fl oz) Scottish gin*
- *75ml (2½fl oz) vermouth*
- *125ml (4fl oz) water*
- *Pared lemon zest, to decorate*

Pour all the ingredients into an empty gin bottle, give it a wee shake to combine, then screw the lid on and place in the freezer overnight. The added water is enough to replicate the loosening you get when making a martini from scratch, but is not enough for the liquid to freeze solid.

To serve, pop your glasses into the freezer to chill, then pour the martini straight in. Decorate with a strip of lemon zest, spritzed over the top.

Smoky Martini

I love a martini. Even though a classic dry martini with a twist is our favourite, my husband and I like to play around with the flavours. Adding whisky instead of vermouth opens up a new world – you can take the profile any direction you want, from smoky to sweet.

Serves 1

- *60ml (4 tablespoons) Scottish dry gin*
- *10–15ml (2–3 teaspoons) single malt whisky*
- *Ice*
- *Pared strip of lemon zest, to decorate*

Pour the spirits into a cocktail shaker filled with ice. I like it quite loose, so shake, then rest, give a gentle swirl, then shake again. Pour into a chilled martini glass and decorate with a freshly pared strip of lemon zest.

Glasgow Punch

Here's my modern twist on a popular Glasgow cocktail, made famous in the middle of the 19th century when the trade routes between Glasgow and the West Indies were at a high.

Serves 1

- *Ice*
- *60ml (4 tablespoons) Scottish spiced rum*
- *30ml (2 tablespoons) homemade Lime Cordial (see page 208)*
- *1 lemon wedge*
- *Sparkling water, to top up*

To decorate

- *1 cinnamon stick*
- *Pared strip of lemon zest*

Add a scoop of ice to a tumbler and pour over the rum and lime cordial. Squeeze in the juice from the lemon wedge and top up with sparkling water. Stir and add a cinnamon stick and a strip of lemon zest as a decoration.

Glasgow Kiss

Glasgow is a vibrant city that is brimming with character, warmth and creativity. While it is celebrated for its rich cultural spirit, it also carries a historic reputation for toughness. Playing on that contrast, this cocktail's name is slang for a headbutt. Thankfully, this version shouldn't leave you with a headache. It's a delightful wee sip with festive, Christmassy notes and a gentle spicy kick.

Serves 1

- *60ml (4 tablespoons) Scottish spiced rum*
- *60ml (4 tablespoons) tangerine or mandarin juice*
- *1 tablespoon ginger syrup or cordial*
- *Few drops of orange bitters*
- *1 tablespoon egg white*
- *½ teaspoon orange marmalade (optional)*
- *Ice*

To decorate

- *Pared strip of tangerine zest*
- *Grating of nutmeg*

Place all the liquid ingredients and marmalade (if using) into a cocktail shaker filled with ice and give a good hard shake. Strain out the ice and shake again, then strain into a chilled martini glass. Decorate with a twist of tangerine zest and a grating of nutmeg.

My Atholl Brose

Originally thought to have been invented in 1475 by the Earl of Atholl, legend of this Scottish cocktail goes further back than that! In a bid to defeat a Highland rebellion, the Earl of Atholl was said to have filled a well that the rebels drank from with oats, honey and whisky. After quenching their thirst, the inebriated rebels were then easier to capture!

Despite the stories, and unlikely ingredients, this is really a very pleasant drink, and if you are a fan of Irish Baileys, as I am, then you will love this homemade Scottish version. You can mix it all together and leave in the refrigerator, but I like to serve it more like a cocktail float, allowing guests to stir before drinking. The coffee liqueur is an addition, but well worth it – it really brings the flavours together.

For the honey simple syrup (makes 300ml/10fl oz)

- *200g (7oz) runny honey*
- *100ml (3½fl oz) hot water*

For the toasted oat milk (makes 600ml/20fl oz)

- *150g (5½oz) fine-ground oatmeal (you can use rolled oats)*
- *600ml (20fl oz) whole milk*

Serves 1

- *Ice*
- *30ml (2 tablespoons) blended whisky*
- *15ml (1 tablespoon) coffee liqueur*
- *15ml (1 tablespoon) honey simple syrup (see above)*
- *60ml (4 tablespoons) toasted oat milk (see above), plus extra if needed*

To serve (optional)

- *Whipped cream*
- *Sprinkle of freshly grated nutmeg*

For the honey simple syrup, pour the honey and hot water into a bottle, stir, then shake until the honey has dissolved. Let it cool, then it's ready to use. Shelf stable, this will keep for ages to use in any cocktails, herbal tea or baking.

For the toasted oat milk, toast the oatmeal in a dry pan until it smells toasty and is starting to change colour. Transfer to a lidded bowl, leave to cool, then pour the milk over. Give it a good stir, pop the lid on and refrigerate overnight. Next day, strain through a muslin or very fine sieve. Save the soaked oats for breakfast.

To make the cocktail

Half-fill a small tumbler with ice. Pour in the whisky, coffee liqueur and honey simple syrup, and stir well. Pour the toasted oat milk over the back of a spoon down the side of the glass – it should settle at the bottom. Add a swizzle stick and let your guests stir before drinking.

For a warm version, you can add a little more toasted oat milk, then gently heat and serve topped with whipped cream and a sprinkle of fresh nutmeg – delicious.

Sauces and Seasonings

11

My Scottish 5-Spice Blend

There are spices that I keep and use on repeat in my Scottish cakes and bakes, so it made sense to make up a proprietary blend to have on hand at all times. Getting the balance right is key. When I smell this mix, it immediately makes me think of Perkins oat biscuits. It's great to add that heady mix of spice in a single hit and it's so adaptable to any recipe.

Makes 1 small jar

- *4 teaspoons ground cinnamon*
- *4 teaspoons ground ginger*
- *2 teaspoons ground allspice*
- *2 teaspoons ground nutmeg*
- *½ teaspoon ground cloves*

Add everything to a jar, screw on the lid and shake well.

My Scottish 7-Spice Blend

After making so many Scottish recipes over the last few years, I noticed I was using the same herbs and spices on repeat, so I created a blend that represents the essence of Celtic flavours. It is so adaptable, and you will find you are using it for so many things, from marinades to roast potatoes and everything in between.

Makes 1 small jar

- *25g (scant 1oz) black peppercorns*
- *15g (½oz) coriander seeds*
- *1 tablespoon juniper berries*
- *1 tablespoon allspice berries*
- *1 tablespoon dried thyme*
- *1 tablespoon dried rosemary*
- *1 tablespoon ground nutmeg*

Toast the black peppercorns, coriander seeds, juniper and allspice berries in a dry pan until fragrant, then blend to a powder using a spice grinder. Alternatively, you could use a pestle and mortar. Add the thyme and rosemary and blend again. Finally, add the ground nutmeg and blend together.

Decant into a jar and use freely and creatively whenever you want to add a bit of Celtic flavour.

My Scottish 7-Spice Salt

Leave about a teaspoon of the blend in the grinder and add 3 tablespoons of flaked salt. Blend together and you have a Scottish 7-Spice Salt for using with my Scottish 7-Spice Blend or on its own for seasoning with a little bit extra.

Broon Sauce

Broon (brown) sauce is popular in Scotland. It's magic on pies, chips, bridies, morning rolls... you name it, and we'll put broon sauce on it. It's also great as a wee flavour bomb – add it to sauces, mince, stews and gravy.

Makes about 600ml (20fl oz)

- *5 tomatoes*
- *1 bay leaf*
- *1 blade of mace*
- *1 cinnamon stick*
- *8 cloves*
- *8 allspice berries*
- *1 star anise*
- *Drizzle of olive oil*
- *1 brown onion, chopped*
- *40g (1½oz) fresh root ginger, peeled and chopped*
- *4 garlic cloves, chopped*
- *Pinch of salt*
- *2 Granny Smith apples, cored and grated (unpeeled)*
- *1 tablespoon soy sauce*
- *2 tablespoons black treacle*
- *2 tablespoons tamarind paste*
- *1 tablespoon date syrup*
- *125ml (4fl oz) cider vinegar*
- *1 tablespoon brown sugar*

Make a small cross in the bottom of each tomato, then place in a bowl and cover with boiling water. Drain, then peel off the skins, deseed and roughly chop. Set aside, reserving the juices released.

Place the bay leaf and whole spices in a piece of muslin and tie into a bag with a piece of kitchen string. This is your bouquet garni. Set aside.

Heat the olive oil in a saucepan, add the onion, ginger and garlic with a pinch of salt and start to soften. When soft, add the chopped tomatoes with their juices and the grated apple along with with the bouquet garni. Add the soy sauce, treacle, tamarind paste and date syrup followed by the cider vinegar. Stir, cover and let it simmer for about 30 minutes.

After this time, add the brown sugar and simmer for a further 5 minutes.

Remove the bouquet garni and blitz the mixture to a purée. Push through a sieve, then decant into sterilized bottles. Store in the refrigerator to use on anything you fancy. It will keep for 3 months.

Tommy K

Tomato ketchup was my preferred sauce as a child. Until very recently, I hadn't even tried brown sauce! I still love ketchup on my Tattie Scone and Bacon Piece (see page 22). This homemade version is delicious. Fresh tomatoes are simmered down to a thick, intensely flavoured, spiced sauce, ready to liven up your breakfast, lunch and dinner.

Makes about 500ml (18fl oz)

- *1kg (2lb 4oz) tomatoes, roughly chopped*
- *6 garlic cloves, roughly chopped*
- *1 onion, roughly chopped*
- *1 Granny Smith apple, cored and roughly chopped (unpeeled)*
- *1 bird's eye chilli*
- *1 cinnamon stick*
- *1 bay leaf*
- *½ teaspoon ground mace*
- *10 allspice berries*
- *1 teaspoon coriander seeds*
- *4 cloves*
- *5 juniper berries*
- *100g (3½oz) soft brown sugar*
- *100g (3½oz) apple cider vinegar*
- *1 teaspoon salt, or to taste*
- *Xanthan gum (0.5% of final weight)*

In a blender or food processor, combine the tomatoes, garlic, onion, apple and chilli and blend to a purée.

Transfer the mixture to a saucepan and add the cinnamon stick, bay leaf and mace. Place the allspice, coriander seeds, cloves and juniper berries in a small piece of muslin and tie into a bag with kitchen string. Add to the pan. Simmer gently for 30 minutes with the lid on.

After this time, add the brown sugar and vinegar and simmer for another 30 minutes, stirring occasionally.

Remove the spice bag, cinnamon stick and bay leaf, and transfer the sauce to a blender. Blend until smooth, then season with the salt, adjusting to taste. Strain through a sieve back into the saucepan and simmer uncovered until the sauce has thickened.

To finish, weigh your sauce, then sprinkle over 0.5% of the total weight in Xanthan gum. Blend thoroughly with a handheld immersion blender. Decant into sterilized bottles and store in the refrigerator. It will keep for 3 months.

Punchy Parsley Sauce

We always had parsley growing in our garden at home so Mum would garnish everything with it! This is a way to use this herb for more, it adds a real hit of flavour to soups, stews and roasts. Particularly good with my Pressed Lamb (see page 94).

Serves 8

- *Handful of parsley, finely chopped*
- *Zest of 1 lemon*
- *1 garlic clove, crushed*
- *Pinch of salt*
- *Good-quality olive oil, as needed*

Mix all the ingredients in a small bowl and add enough olive oil to create a drizzling consistency. You can make this ahead of time to let the flavours infuse.

Gin-and-Tonic Pickled Onions

I pickle red onions a lot. I love them on anything from toasties to tacos, cheeseboards to burgers...you will often find a jar in my refrigerator. They are so easy to make and better than shop-bought. Try this little twist using Scottish gin and tonic. I have added some gin-forward spices, like coriander and juniper, but also fresh herbs, and these all contribute to a superior flavoured pickle.

Makes 1 × 1 litre (1¾ pint) jar

- *1 teaspoon juniper berries*
- *1 teaspoon coriander seeds*
- *1 teaspoon allspice berries*
- *1 teaspoon mixed peppercorns*
- *100ml (3½fl oz) Scottish gin*
- *200ml (7fl oz) white wine vinegar*
- *200ml (7fl oz) tonic water*
- *100g (3½oz) granulated sugar*
- *1 teaspoon salt*
- *1 bay leaf*
- *2 sprigs of thyme*
- *2 large pieces of pared lemon zest*
- *1 large garlic clove, peeled*
- *4 red onions*

Put the whole spices into a hot, dry pan and roast them for a few minutes until fragrant. Add the gin to the hot pan and let it simmer for a minute or so, then add the vinegar, tonic water, sugar, salt, herbs, lemon zest and garlic. Leave over a low heat until the sugar has dissolved, then turn the heat off.

Finely slice the onions. A mandoline is ideal to get them super thin, but a sharp knife will also do the job. Stuff them into a large sterilized jar and pour the hot pickling liquid on top. Leave to cool to room temperature, then refrigerate.

You can eat these within a few hours, but ideally you should leave them for a couple of days until the liquid turns pink. They are best eaten within a month and will happily go on any cheeseboard, on Tattie Scone Tacos (see page 106), on Confit Sardines (see page 59) or anywhere you need a little pickle in your life.

Carrot Top and Mint Sauce

This punchy wee sauce makes the most of the tops on new-season carrots that may get thrown away. Pound them up with mint and garlic and it makes a fabulous addition to any lamb dish, particularly my Hotch Potch (see page 63). You can even use it to dress the carrots from which the tops came.

- *2 garlic cloves*
- *1 tablespoon chopped carrot tops*
- *1 tablespoon chopped mint leaves*
- *1 egg yolk*
- *Squeeze of lemon juice*
- *1 teaspoon Dijon mustard*
- *75ml (2½fl oz) light olive oil*
- *Salt*

Pound the garlic in a pestle and mortar until crushed, add a good pinch of salt and the carrot tops, then continue to pound. Add the mint and pound again until a smooth green paste is achieved. Add the egg yolk, lemon juice and mustard. While mixing in a circular motion, start drizzling in the olive oil, stirring all the while until a smooth, thick emulsion is formed. Chill in the refrigerator until ready to use.

Whisky Mac Hot Sauce

This is a fiery green hot sauce with the gentle smokiness of whisky. Try it on anything where you need a bit of heat, from tacos to eggs to roast chicken! It's really fabulous with my Macaroni Pies (see page 35) and Tattie Scone Tacos (see page 106).

Makes about 600ml (20fl oz)

- *1 onion*
- *4 garlic cloves*
- *Thumb-sized piece of fresh root ginger, peeled*
- *3 jalapeño chillies*
- *3 green cayenne chillies*
- *1 teaspoon light olive oil*
- *60ml (4 tablespoons) smoky Scottish whisky, plus a splash to finish*
- *60ml (4 tablespoons) green ginger wine*
- *350g (12oz) green tomatoes*
- *20g (¾oz) flat-leaf parsley*
- *1 tablespoon caster sugar*
- *60ml (4 tablespoons) white vinegar*
- *½ teaspoon salt, or to taste*

Blitz the onion, garlic, ginger and chillies together in a food processor, or chop finely by hand.

Heat the oil in a small pan, add the blitzed mixture and sauté until softened, then add the whisky and green ginger wine and let the alcohol bubble off.

With the same processor or blender, blitz the tomatoes and parsley to a purée, then add to the pan along with the sugar and vinegar. Taste and season with salt. Simmer for 10–15 minutes.

Transfer to a blender and purée until smooth. I finish with another drop of smoky whisky, then pour into a sterilized bottle and leave to cool. Store in the refrigerator – it's good for up to a month.

Whisky Hot Honey

I have been guilty of buying hot honey, but it has often left me disappointed with the level of heat, so I finally decided to make my own and it couldn't be easier. This way you can make it how you like it: mild or super-hot. Add herbs, spices or even a smoky note with some whisky.

Makes about 350g (12oz)

- *350g (12oz) nice local honey*
- *1½ tablespoons red chilli flakes*
- *1 heaped teaspoon My Scottish 7-Spice Blend (see page 214)*
- *1½ tablespoons whisky*

Add the honey, chilli flakes and spices to a saucepan and heat gently, just enough so the honey becomes viscous. Add the whisky, then turn off the heat. Leave to infuse for 15 minutes, then either pour into a sterilized jar or strain into a squeezy bottle for ease of use.

You can try it on everything: drizzle on sausage rolls, pasta, eggs... It also makes a great addition to a salad dressing.

Whisky Onion Jam

This is a versatile condiment that keeps you going back for more. It's brilliant warmed up on sausage and mash, with haggis, neeps and tatties, or if you fancy something different with your roll and square sausage for breakfast.

Makes about 350g (12oz)

- *2 tablespoons neutral oil*
- *2 brown onions, thinly sliced*
- *6 garlic cloves, finely sliced*
- *1 bay leaf*
- *Small bunch of thyme*
- *1 tablespoon granulated sugar*
- *60ml (4 tablespoons) blended whisky*
- *60ml (4 tablespoons) soy sauce*
- *Splash of Worcestershire sauce (or balsamic vinegar, if you are vegetarian or vegan)*
- *500ml (18fl oz) vegetable stock*
- *60ml (4 tablespoons) barbecue sauce (or brown sauce)*
- *Splash of sherry vinegar*

Heat the oil in a saucepan over a medium heat and cook down the onions and garlic with the bay leaf and thyme until soft and starting to turn golden.

Add the sugar and stir until starting to caramelize, then add the whisky and let it bubble down.

Add the soy sauce, Worcestershire sauce and stock, then add the barbecue sauce. Stir to combine and let it reduce until most of the liquid has gone.

Add a splash of sherry vinegar and reduce a little further until it looks jammy. Decant into a jar. It will keep for a month in the refrigerator.

I think this is best served warmed slightly, but even if left at room temperature on a cheeseboard it's perfect.

Jam with a Dram

Raspberry jam features heavily in Scottish recipes – perhaps because when they are in season, Scottish raspberries are just about the best you will ever taste! I'd often go raspberry picking with my mum, usually eating more than I collected. I have used this jam on everything from my Paradise Slice (see page 176) to my Selkirk Bannock (see page 161). Try replacing the raspberries with strawberries and a shot of Scottish gin.

Makes 1 jar

- *400g (14oz) raspberries*
- *400g (14oz) caster sugar*
- *Juice of 1 lemon*
- *40ml (2½ tablespoons) blended whisky*

Add the raspberries, sugar and lemon juice to a small pan, then squish together with a clean hand. You could wear plastic food-safe gloves if you prefer. Bring to the boil, then simmer until thickened, stirring occasionally. You can test whether it has reached the setting point by dropping a little on a freezer-cold saucer. It should wrinkle when pushed with the tip of your finger.

Remove it from the heat and add the whisky. It will bubble furiously while you stir it and boil off the alcohol. Decant into a sterilized jar and get ready to liven up your scones.

This jam will keep for a year unopened and 6 months when opened.

Index

Glossary

Scottish Glossary

bacon piece – bacon sandwich
bannocks – unyeasted flatbreads
bridies – meat pasties/pies
neeps – swede
skirlie – fried oatmeal
stovies – potato-based stew
supper – something served with chips from the chip shop
tatties – potatoes

UK/US Glossary

baking tin – baking pan
baking tray – baking sheet
barbecue – grill
beetroot/s – beet/s
bicarbonate of soda – baking soda
biscuits – cookies
butter beans – lima beans
cake tin – cake pan
casserole dish – Dutch oven
caster sugar – superfine sugar
chickpea flour – besan
chilli/chillies – chili/chiles
chilli flakes – red pepper flakes
chips – French fries
clingfilm – plastic wrap
coriander (fresh) – cilantro
cornflour – cornstarch
crisps – chips
Demerara sugar – turbinado sugar
double cream – heavy cream
filo pastry – phyllo pastry
frying pan – skillet
golden syrup – corn syrup
grill – broil/broiler
icing – frosting
icing sugar – confectioners' powdered sugar
king prawn – jumbo shrimp
kitchen foil – aluminum foil
kitchen paper – paper towels
minced meat – ground meat
muslin – cheesecloth
natural yogurt – plain yogurt
plain flour – all-purpose flour
prawn – shrimp
rapeseed oil – canola oil
roasting tin – roasting pan
self-raising flour – self-rising flour
semi-skimmed milk – half-fat milk
sieve – strainer
spring onions – scallions
starter – appetizer
stock – broth
sultanas – golden raisins
swede – rutabaga
tea towel – dish towel
tomato purée – tomato paste
treacle – molasses
whole milk – full-fat milk
wholemeal – wholewheat

First published in Great Britain in 2026
by Mitchell Beazley, an imprint of
Octopus Publishing Group Ltd
Carmelite House
50 Victoria Embankment
London EC4Y 0DZ
www.octopusbooks.co.uk

An Hachette UK Company
www.hachette.co.uk

The authorized representative in the EEA is Hachette Ireland, 8 Castlecourt Centre, Dublin 15, D15 XTP3, Ireland (email: info@hbgi.ie)

Distributed in the US by Hachette Book Group, 1290 Avenue of the Americas, 4th and 5th Floors, New York, NY 10104

Distributed in Canada by Canadian Manda Group, 664 Annette St, Toronto, Ontario, Canada M6S 2C8

ISBN: 978-1-84601-648-6
eISBN: 978-1-84601-649-3

A CIP catalogue record for this book is available from the British Library.

Printed and bound in China.

10 9 8 7 6 5 4 3 2 1

Commissioning Editor: Jeannie Stanley
Creative Director: Jonathan Christie
Senior Editor: Leanne Bryan
Copyeditor: Emily Preece-Morrison
Food Photographer: Sally Hulse
Styling: Ali Stoner and Sally Hulse
Book Designer: Ali Stoner
Production Controllers:
Lucy Carter and Nic Jones

MIX
Paper | Supporting responsible forestry
FSC www.fsc.org FSC® C008047

Ali Stoner or 'Roving Haggis' as she is known on social media, is a highly creative Scottish cook, previous Masterchef Australia contestant and social media influencer. Born in Glasgow, she currently lives in Melbourne, Australia, with her husband and two children.

An art school graduate, Ali spent her early career in London's creative industry and was a partner in a leading retail design agency until 2008. In 2011, following a career break, she moved to Australia with her family, and continued on her creative journey as an artist with a number of successful exhibitions, primarily using glass as a medium.

In early 2022, encouraged by her friends and family, she was finally tempted to stretch her cooking talents further and applied to be a contestant on Masterchef Australia.

During her time on the show, her creativity and inventiveness were a stand out, with the experience encouraging her to take her food journey further, exploring her Scottish heritage. In May 2023, Alison launched her Instagram presence under the 'Roving Haggis' moniker and has seen her audience grow rapidly, with particularly large audiences in North America, Canada, Australia and, of course, Scotland and the UK.

Acknowledgements

The list of thanks is enormous, as putting this book together has affected everyone in my orbit, so I thank you all for your patience and continuous love.

To my social-media following, this book has been made because of your likes, follows and shares. My heart is full with your support and kind words.

Specifically, a special thanks to the following people...

Marion Lawson, Mum: For being my teacher and inspiration. I am forever grateful for everything I learned from you... and, of course, for your recipes!

Norman Lawson, Dad: You have always believed in me, have never questioned my choices and have always been my biggest fan.

Euan Lawson, my brother, friend (and lawyer!): Thanks for the advice, patience and support, and for always having my back.

Steve Stoner, my husband, my best friend, my rock: You have the patience of a saint, the heart of an angel... and you're an expert martini maker!

Evie Stoner: Thank you for letting your old mum dominate the kitchen for so long when all you wanted to do was make cookies.

Maggie Stoner, my social-media expert: Thanks for keeping your influencer mum on track!

Sally Hulse, my fantastic food photographer, stylist and total legend: It's scary how our minds were so often thinking the same thing. It made a very hard couple of weeks a whole lot easier!

Jo Fletcher, Joseppi, my 'chef de plonge', dog walker extraordinaire and one of my top 17: What a legend of a pal and cleaner-upper you are!

The Octopus team: Thanks to you all for believing in me, and for all the support, guidance and help to make this dream of mine a reality.

Finally to Scotland: A land full of history, food, love, laughter, tradition, language, islands, mountains, fresh air and the best water in the world. My birthright and lifetime of inspiration.